Virtually Painless

The Reality of Moving from PA to VA, Employee to Business Owner

Kathy Soulsby

CONTENTS

Foreword by Charlotte Wibberley

I'm so excited to see this book on the market! I think it will be a great read for anyone who is thinking of making the leap from being employed to being a Virtual Assistant. I work with many people going through this transition and having a fresh, honest and funny look at the reality of the experience can only be a good thing. This book does spell it out – the good, the bad and ugly.

When you first dip your toe in the water of this world, a simple internet search will drive you crazy. The vast swathes of information out there can be totally overwhelming. You need an authentic, true and relatable view of what it can be like; how it can feel, the types of things you will now need to do, what skills you'll need and where to find help if it all gets too much. You also need to decide if it is right for you – the freelance life really isn't for everyone.

The VA industry is bigger and more exciting than ever, particularly in the UK. But, with scale comes the challenge of keeping standards high. Anyone can set themselves up as a VA but not everyone can set themselves up as a good VA. I've worked with Kathy for some time now and spoken to her clients – she is a truly great VA and her clients have testified to that in spades! Her enthusiasm and passion for the industry and what she does shine through, even as you are laughing at the various hilarious scrapes she has got into on her journey. She may be incredibly funny but she is also deadly serious about giving her clients an amazing service. I suspect most of them probably do have a laugh with her along the way though. In my eyes, she is the ideal person to have written this book.

As an introduction to the industry, this is a book I would encourage anyone thinking about becoming a VA to read. I thoroughly enjoyed every page and I hope you will too.

Charlotte

Charlotte Wibberley, Founder, VIP VA

Charlotte set up her award-winning VA business after leaving a long blue chip corporate career following the birth of her son in 2012. She then went on to launch her online business management and strategy consultancy in early 2015.

Charlotte launched VIP VA in January 2016 keen to support, nurture and champion the VA industry, and to create a safe space for high performing VA businesses to collaborate, knowledge share and continue their professional development. She supports aspiring and existing VAs as their coach, mentor and chief-cheerleader for their goals and ambitions. Founder and CEO of VIP VA, Charlotte is currently on a mission to improve industry standards and engage with VAs and business owners alike around the true value of the VA and worth that they bring.

@vipvaorg

@CharlotteWibb

PROLOGUE

If you'd have told me five years ago, that in the future I would leave a perfectly nice and secure job to go and set up my own business I would have been rolling on the floor in hysterics. Me? Me so risk averse and wimpy I can't ride roller coasters and thought I'd nearly died of fear on the walzer once in my early twenties (I was on a date, not sure that lying on the floor nearly sobbing in terror was ideal but we did go out for a while, must have been a good bonding experience?). Wimpy me? Nah! Not a hope. That wild crazy stuff is for other people. I'm just a PA... *

But freakishly, here I am. Running a little business. On my own. (Well, kind of, more on that later, I have been helped, supported and backed up all the way). And I am loving it.

This book is not about how to set up and work as a VA – there are many books, courses and online resources for those that want and need that. I didn't use any of those, I just hurled myself at it and was lucky enough to have some great friends and VA mentors to ring when the gung-ho approach left a little to be desired.

This is a light-hearted look at what it is actually like to do it. Warts and all. The highs, the lows, the "oh-dear-God-why-did-no-bastard-tell-me?"s. It is a personal account of my experience, which is compared to many, very limited. But I hope it's a fun read and gives you an insight into a world that you might not otherwise come across. I still have loads to learn and plenty to experience, but so far, it's been virtually painless....

* Please note, there is no such thing as "Just a PA". I did know that at the time. I still know it now, but somehow, I never felt it carried enough gravitas in my mind. "Just a PA" was kind of a thing for me. Every PA I have ever known has basically been the glue that holds the company together. If you ever need to know how key a PA is, check the colour on the boss' face when they head off for a holiday, it's somewhere between grey and corpse-white as they say bravely through gritted teeth "have a lovely time" knowing that it'll be the hardest two weeks of their working year and they will probably cry at least three times.

WHY WOULD YOU DO THIS?

People decide to go freelance for all types of reasons. Sometimes they are sick of corporate life and can't bear the thought of another meeting, maybe they want more time at home with their kids, partner or to get a horse or a dog. Or maybe they just got made redundant and are seeing this as the perfect opportunity to try something new. Whatever the reason, it will probably not be what they think!

I can't actually remember the first time I said to myself "I could be one of those there Virtual Assistant things". I do know that the first time I did think about it in any great seriousness I managed to be talked out of it by someone who was completely dismissive of my ability to do it. And back in those days of employment and misery my self-esteem was so low that I basically said "Oh. Yes. I'm sure you're right, I won't do it then" and completely dismissed the idea. As you can tell, I'm hardly a budding Richard Branson if at the first hurdle I'm talked out of it by someone who, frankly, I should never have listened to!

But the idea wouldn't leave me. It kept niggling along. I'd just hit forty. In fact, as I'd been telling everyone I was thirty-two for eight years I hadn't so much hit forty as have forty hit me really fecking hard. Reality

3

bites. My job was going nowhere. My self-esteem was in the toilet after years of being micro-managed, I couldn't so much as decide on a font size without a twenty-minute internal agonise over which one would be wrong (which was pointless; the answer was whichever one I picked would be wrong because I'd have analysed myself into such a flap I'd have accidently managed to turn it into Arial when it should have been Calibri). This is not an enjoyable way to live, I decided. I need to get out of here before I end up in Tesco having a panic attack unable to decide on a type of Flora.

It was at this point I blatantly picked the brains of a VA I knew a little bit who lived locally. We went out for a dog walk and I mercilessly interrogated her about how it worked, what it is like and how on earth she found clients. All that stuff. She really made it sound quite easy and kindly invited me to a local event with even more VAs where I could leech yet more information. It was a revelation. All these people doing this! All these normal people, like me, doing this and managing to pay the mortgage and go out for hot chocolate in the middle of the day! Oh, I was loving this.

My next stop was an accountant friend of my dads' who, along with a group of local businesses, has been a huge support. She gave me blow by blow account of what to do to set up. Which took moments. It was largely filling in an online form at HMRC to register as self-employed. And then apparently, I was officially in business...

How does it all work then?

"Well, it's just like being a freelance PA…"

I love being a VA and would genuinely recommend it if you think you have the right skills and mindset. But it may not be what you expect….

When I decided, more or less on a whim, to try this VA malarkey, I really thought that as a PA it was just a matter of working in a different way, freelancing instead of being employed. And on paper this is entirely the case. However, the reality is that I didn't have a CLUE! Not a Scooby about how different it would be. There are a million ways in which working for yourself is different. Some are, without doubt amazing (working in PJs, getting to have a dog, not having an actual boss, going to the gym at 10am and so forth). But some are really hard. Really hard. This book is a very brief summary of the "oh God I wish I'd twigged that" moments that I have had since making the transition.

Your boss may be the most demanding git in the world and may give you deadlines that are insane but you can talk to him about all the work you have on your plate and how unreasonable that is (or go to HR and cry if that's your preferred option!). As a freelancer, you'll probably have four or five clients at any one time. And none of them want to know about the others or how busy they are making you. They really don't.

And, FYI, this isn't just a PA to VA thing. I've met HR consultants who were previously in corporate life and decided to go it alone, they have the same pain. Probably more money in their back pockets to buffer it, but the same pain!

You are now running a business. With all that entails. Plus, the work is different. Yup. All those shit hot PA skills I have, juggling insane diaries, booking mental travel schedules all totally unused. The kind of clients I have just don't want that kind of support and conversations with other VAs would seem to validate this. Running a diary as a VA is very, very different and actually, the one time I did try it as a VA I quit after a week. On the hours I was booked it was totally impossible to provide the cover needed ("can you cancel that meeting in an hour?" and other last minute requests that are totally doable as an employee are really not workable as a VA). That thing you have when you are a PA or EA, and you know every move your boss makes and precisely where he'll be at any given moment is a real hard one to pull off as a VA because it is so time consuming. How many times did I look at that diary in a day, lots, may be twenty even thirty times if I was booking lots of meetings. How often did I get calls or emails to book or move things? Loads. It just isn't cost effective for many clients to have that level of cover. Some VAs do it, but not as many as you might think. That's the downside. The upside is that as well as the pile of usual admin things that are more junior than I might have done as a PA/EA after a time I have become in many ways a more respected outsourced colleague and do much more advisory work. Being paid for my opinions!

No work, no money. Yeah yeah, redundancy money. It doesn't last forever. There will come a point where no matter how many networking meetings you haul yourself to, no one is biting. The few leads you have fizzle into nothing and you have to keep motivating yourself and getting out there even when you are pretty convinced it's all pointless and you might as well just stack shelves in Tesco. And what about when you're ill? Or want a holiday? Or someone in the family is ill and you have to drop everything? Or just can't be fagged to get out of bed because it's all too hard? I knew this intellectually, of course I did, I'm no muppet. But how it feels is scary. And even when you do have work, most VAs work based on client billable time so literally, you can sit at your desk for ten hours and only be paid for five. Trust me, it happens!

"Hello, IT? My Outlook seems to have frozen". As a freelancer, you are now the boss. Hurrah. However, you are now also the IT Department, Sales Department, Marketing Department, Finance Department …. Everything. All you. If your laptop dies (or a puppy hurls it onto the floor and kills it dead) not only do you have to get it fixed or replaced, likely you are earning no money until this is done. You can of course have others to do your IT, book-keeping, social media etc. and I have some great suppliers, but they all cost money and, especially with IT or broadband, they may not be very timely when you are under pressure. After the puppy incident I was simultaneously on the phone to my IT guys and climbing on a ladder to get my 2005 desktop out of the attic trying hard not to hyperventilate. FYI I now have two set ups – a desktop and a laptop, it's that vital that I can't be without something to work on.

"So, you answer the phone then?" People just don't get it

Love 'em. These are the ones that have not the faintest idea what a VA does. Which is fine if they are willing to learn. But some just don't get it. And it's usually the ones I meet face to face at meetings. Who do they think is answering the phone if I am with them? My invisible friend?

There has always been a tendency to look down on those working in support roles. As if somehow, they are less than. And this has drifted through to the role of VA for some people. They really think that the sum total of what we can do is a bit of typing and answering the phone. They usually shut up fairly fast when I tell them that answering the phone is in fact the one thing I don't do (there are loads of things I hate and try to avoid doing, don't get me wrong – complex travel arrangements, personal work like insurances and booking gardeners, personal party planning, anything involving stupidly rich people really – but actually upfront state I DON'T do – phone answering and book-keeping!) and then if they look like a dinosaur technophobe I'll chuck in some phrases like "Setting up CRM systems, back office support and social media management" just to fry their noodles a bit.

I had one just now as I am writing this! A random German man staying in a room I let out on Air BnB (Air BNB – a whole other book of weird people and freakish experiences!) ambled into my office to say, "good morning" and "do I have a card?". His son runs a hotel in Spain and needs someone to speak to his English customers. "I don't take calls". Do people not think? How is one person meant to take calls for multiple businesses? Do I have call centre tattooed on my head? He'd been in my house two days and probably only heard me on the phone twice and one of those times was my mother…

There are specialist services which focus purely on call answering and they are actually a load more cost efficient than a VA would be because they are set up with shifts, the right pricing and the right equipment and they are good at what they do. So, I tend to refer people straight on to them without worrying that they may have taken on more services from me. In my experience, the kind of company that relies on phone calls being answered straight away isn't right for me anyway because of my niche clients. Those that need company calls picking up tend to be "instant purchase / book now" work - trades like electricians, plumbers (tree surgeons!), or beauty therapy or whatever. Anyone buying consultancy or coaching (my main niche), is highly unlikely to be fazed by getting a voicemail, it's going to take weeks of sales to get to a buy point so getting a call back a few hours later is neither here nor there. So, my ideal clients really aren't worried about having any kind of call coverage.

Once I have explained to people what it is I do when I am busy *not* answering the phone, they look differently at me. But is it hard to describe in terms of tasks as they are so varied. And although I am sure that the tasks I do are the main reason people need me, the reason people stay with me is because I'm a partner with them in their business, working alongside them to make their business the best it can be. And that is valuable for small businesses that don't have teams as such, or the teams are so frantic they don't have time to think about streamlining their back-office processes. Anyway, I digress. I don't answer the fucking phone.

Ad Hoc fly-by-nights – pay as you go work

So, this is how most VAs start I think. Someone asks you to do some work, you do it, they pay you.

Obviously, it is a little more complex than this but that's the gist. There is no commitment of regular work, no discounts for such and normally (for me anyway) the invoice is sent either monthly if it is ongoing or at the end of the piece of work.

Pure Ad Hoc work is a one-off job for someone. Some VAs charge for this upfront, or take a deposit, especially if this is someone they don't know. Sometimes clients want a quote and sometimes they just want the work done and it takes as long as it takes. So far, so flaky! But the idea of this is that it is totally flexible so it covers all eventualities.

It is possible to have "regulars" who are officially Ad Hoc – so you work for them every month but they might use different amounts. I have one chap who almost always comes in between six and eight hours a month. I have another who some months, has no work for me but one month had a huge project that between me and an associate was a hundred odd hours (and, yes, I was very tired).

Retainers – the good, the bad, the ugly

Retainers are normally monthly. They are also thought of as blocks of time. So, a client buys a block of twenty hours, say, for that month.

The advantages of this are that it is guaranteed work. A contract would normally accompany this and it usually has a cancellation period. So, you know that X client will be paying you X amount each month. That's the good bit. Very often they also pay this upfront as well.

By way of thanks for the guaranteed hours and an upfront payment, the hourly rate is normally discounted. By how much might depend on the number of hours. I don't offer any discount for less than a ten-hour block.

Some VAs charge their standard rate if clients go over their fixed hours. Some don't, they just get charged the same discounted amount. The logic is of course that to aid planning, it helps to know how many hours they need. If your client is only committing to ten hours a month but is actually using 35 consistently that's hard to manage, so you gently penalise them by charging extra for the twenty-five they go over, in the hope that they will commit to a more realistic amount.

I find it much more difficult when clients don't use up all their allotted hours. It depends on the contract whether unused hours can be carried over the next month. Some do, some don't, some of us (ahem!) are deeply pathetic when it comes to difficult conversations so end up doing it despite what the contract states... In theory, a client pays for X hours a month, whether or not they use them. In reality, a little give and take isn't a bad thing. For example, what happens when you want a holiday? Can I really fit all my client's committed hours into two weeks instead of four? What happens when they go on holiday? Or get quiet? My contract does say they have to be used but I do tend, in exceptional circumstances to let them roll over into the next month. Just once! If it happens a few times then we need to review how many hours are held on retainer, it's better to drop them and overshoot than have them in the bank causing me sleepless nights.

Retained hours involve a bit more administration and management. With retained clients, I typically send a mid-month timesheet so they can see how many hours they have left. I tend not to with Ad Hoc even those I work with month in, month out. Some clients are more interested than others in the mechanics – most of mine tend to be of the "it takes what it takes" mindset on hours but I have worked with others who really needed know quite exactly and regularly what their hourly use was. Happily, my lovely timesheet system has a "client view" so any client that needs to can look and instantly see where I am at.

Hours and the agony of billable time

I am Minute Dock's Bitch. To the uninitiated, Minute Dock is my current timesheet software. There are many others. I like Minute Dock, they are Kiwis and will gently abuse you if you don't record any time during any given day. I like software that amuses me.

I talk a lot about how people don't get the whole "Not working, not earning" thing, the billable hours' concept takes some getting used to. It really does. I have been known to holler at people that come into the room "I'm on the clock!" because when I am on client work, I am head down, 100% focused on client work.

In day, my diary looks insane because at the start of each week, I chunk my client work up to make sure I have enough time for everything. So, if all goes according to plan, I will clock into Client A at 9am, work on various tasks and emails for that client until 10am then clock out. I then clock into Client B and repeat. Of course, we do not live in an ideal world. While I am mid A, I may have had a message from Client C with something I have been waiting for urgently so I'll clock out of A, into C, make a quick call, clock back into A and so it goes on. The day will involve a lot of clicking in and out of stuff. I try to avoid it but it is pretty inevitable. Making tea, someone at the door, quick loo break all involve a click out and back in again. Then you check your emails which should take two minutes but never seems to and then reply, adding another five minutes. All in all, it is very possible to "work" an eight-hour day and only be paid for five because you end up with ten minutes here, five minutes there and it is all very bitty.

How many billable hours you do becomes an obsession. I have Minute Dock graphs, I have charts, I have daily, weekly and monthly targets. If my "weekly billable hours" tracker is under at any point in the week my stress levels rise quite considerably. I will grab anyone who works in the same way I do (mainly lawyers) and shamelessly bug them for what they think is a reasonable number of billable hours, how many is enough? What about time spent doing internal work? Do you clock off if you go for a wee? How about making a brew? How many hours would a junior lawyer do? I am a woman on the edge when it comes to these things. I read in awe about new lawyers joining USA law firms from college and how they are expected to bill two-hundred hours a month. In a four-week month that is fifty hours a week, ten hours a day. And that doesn't mean they rock up at 8am and finish at 6pm because, as we know, just being in the building isn't billable! In order to hit those targets, they might as well sleep there and work every weekend! I kid you not, those poor bastards do not have lives. I work a typical Monday – Friday 9am – 5.30pm ish with some over here and there and my target monthly hours are around a hundred (twenty-five ish a week). As I say, I've done more, I've done less but certainly what you can't do is work 9am – 5pm with an hour for lunch and expect to earn seven hours. It just doesn't work like that.

And it is a bit bonkers to be so fixated on my charts, but actually, if I don't hit my billable hours I won't earn what I expect to be earning. Having said that, if I do too many billable hours I'm not going to be spending any time doing marketing, networking, sending invoices and so on.

A nice day for me is five billable hours, a kick-ass day is six or more, anything under four without a decent excuse (like I had a meeting or broke a limb) I will feel miserable about. Especially if I have actually been at my desk all day (and it does happen, there is a time-stealing fairy that comes with some clients where you swear to God you have spent a whole frigging day on them and being stressed by them but the total hours add up to three). I have done eight hours and occasionally even ten but I don't recommend doing it often if you value your sanity.

Some clients are more anal about it than others. I've had people tell me that certain tasks shouldn't take longer than seventeen minutes or whatever and that just starts getting mental. You also have to balance billing time with being an OCD twat. I check emails lots, if I am not head down in a particular project, I don't know, say ten times a day ish. I might not **do** anything for a client, there may not be an email in their inbox – do I charge because I checked? Some VAs do. If there is an expectation that an inbox is monitored x times a day then that should be chargeable, right? It may only take two minutes but in that two minutes I could have watched a funny cat video on Facebook. If I don't do anything, I tend to whack five minutes on the clock for "general glancing at mail" the next time I clock on. I only start the clock if I do have to do something. Most clients are very relaxed as long as you are open and honest. And then there are some that would test the patience of Mother Teresa (had she ever had a time tracking system, which isn't likely, but you know what I mean) and send you messages and expect you to be "on" all day and reply but not bill for it. Or you go down the lawyer route and any emails are three minutes each. Or more. Read an email three minutes, reply three minutes.

It's a constant juggling act and an obsession that continues. I knew that I had an issue (and that I am not alone!) when I wondered if I should add a non-billable code to Minute Dock for "fretting about time". I mean I do it, should I at least be tracking how long the agonising takes me and booking it in like I do dog walks!?!? (I don't timesheet them though, promise).

As far as what to bill – everything! If you are talking to a client about work (once they're onboard, obviously) or doing work or planning work or reading emails about the work, it is billable. If you don't bill properly you'll soon discover yourself working all hours and getting paid for a fraction of it.

Niches

"What's your niche?" Ughh. How many times have a read this and seen VA training that is all about your niche? Millions. And people fret their knickers off when they start painfully agonising over ideal clients and the whats and the whys. Well, do you know what? Do it, but don't have a cow over it. I shall start with the cow element...

Any client (that pays!) is a good client. Any client that pays your rate, you like the work and feel like you're making a difference is a bloody brilliant client to have. Why would you decry "you are not my niche client, be gone with you" and hurl them out the window? You wouldn't. Not unless you have a waiting list of better ones or you're a total numpty.

You can work with whoever the hell you want. One of my biggest clients is the most unlikely I could possibly have imagined – you could've given me a list of a thousand types of companies I could work for and this would not be on there. But the work challenges me, they pay me on time, I like them hugely – that's good enough. This does not mean I need to shout about it or go and find others of the same ilk unless it appeals to me. They are unique. In fact, I have three companies I work for that bear no resemblance whatsoever to my ideal client. But I like them. And I am delighted to work with them. If I didn't like them or the work, totally different kettle of fish.

But, it certainly is worth having an ideal client in mind. Even knowing that you'd bite the hand off anyone who ever gives you some work. Why? Well, it keeps you focused.

If you are doing marketing, do you want to be trying to market to everyone from dog groomers to solicitors? You can't possibly want to work with everyone. You have to be able to narrow it down. Do all your target clients hangout in the same places (quite often, the answer is yes!!! Everyone and the dog rocks up to BNI at some point – see the chapter on Networking). It is much easier to think of your ideal client as a specific thing, or collection of things and then you can target them easier.

I'm not going to tell you how to pick you niche. I don't know! And it might be that you have a skills niche (e.g. social media) or an industry niche (e.g. lawyers). Or, you might have both – you can be social media guru to lawyers. Nothing wrong with any approach. The only thing I would say when you pick your niche is do a bit of research into it. I love dogs. Nothing would make me happier than being a VA to a load of dog trainers or walkers or groomers. But, there isn't the margin in their prices for much support and by and large, a lot of what they do is scheduling and bookings so it's a bit dull and therefore I probably wouldn't like it as much as I think I might. For me, it's the same with trades – they want the kind of work I don't really want to do, like phone answering. BUT, if Bill the plumber rocked up tomorrow and was my kind of guy and needed some fun stuff doing, I'd be there in a flash.

Your niche may also be a type of person – working mums, twenty-something entrepreneurs, men with grown up kids, women in marketing. There's no end.

There are lots of VAs out there, so having a niche is an effective way to stand out. But, don't drive yourself nuts about it if you can't think of one straight away, it maybe that you find it as you go along or it may find you.

Onsite Work

For a "virtual" assistant I get out a lot! Like really a lot. I find that I rather enjoy onsite work.

Obviously, it helps if my clients are close-ish. I've yet to do onsite work with my more far-flung clients. But for others, we make it work if we find it helpful.

It's not always joyous, in my early days I did twelve hour days of scanning in what can best be described as a cupboard. This project never seemed to end but at the time, I needed the work and twelve solid billable hours was too good to turn down.

The best thing about onsite work is that you get to spend some really good quality time with your client. There is no doubt that I have the closest relationship with those clients that I have spent face to face time with. You find out more about them and how they work and that is extremely helpful. I'm a great lover of Skype and the like but working together in person really does produce a different kind of dynamic. Also, compared to the normal billing method of ten minutes here and thirty minutes there, typing in "six hours onsite work" is deeply satisfying.

On the downside, you can end up working in places that are worse than any office you've ever been in! Cramped spaces, lightless hell-holes and dubious chairs are but some of the hazards. Then, if you are onsite a lot in a bigger business you have all the client's staff to deal with, which is just weird as a freelancer. You are kind of there, but not there and everyone hates you because they've realised that you earn more than them AND you get to leave when it all gets too much. You have to put on clothes, proper shoes and maybe even make up and then remember not to pull faces for a long period of time.

I've also worked with clients and contacts at my house. This has mixed benefits. Clearly, the travel time is no issue! But, as a non-anal human with two very hairy dogs there is an element of panic and tidying and sweeping and sorting out. And let's not even talk about the time my client and I ended up chasing a mouse out of my house!

Contracts, insurance and other mind-numbingly dull stuff

Just when you though this couldn't get any duller eh? Contracts. In the early days, I did what pretty much everyone does and cobbled something together from various ones I found. Bad move. I mean none have come to bite me or anything but if, God forbid, anything did come up they are probably as water tight as a rusty colander. I now have proper contracts, created especially for VAs, which I do feel much more secure about. It is worth getting this right. They aren't ludicrously expensive to buy from someone reputable – I suggest that you go for VA ones or at worst freelancer ones otherwise they won't be relevant.

Insurance is another dull-but-necessary investment. In our ever more litigious world, you just need to be covered for Professional Indemnity and Public Liability. You also need to make sure that your home and car insurance cover you for working in a new way. Yawn, I know, just suck it up, chances are it won't cost you any more but if you crash the car (or someone crashes into you!) on the way to a sales meeting and you haven't told them, it's a perfect excuse for them not to pay up.

Other extraordinarily dull things to think about: – Money Laundering. Not doing it, registering with HMRC if you do any book-keeping-esque work (and paying them for the privilege) and registering with Data Protection. I'm not going to go into the whys and wherefores. In part because it is so dull I will end up nodding off but largely because this stuff is changing all the time and by 2018 there may be some other bastard thing HMRC expects us to do. This is where VA training is useful – providers should be keeping up with the law and keeping you updated on what, if anything, you need to do. Also, being an active part of UK VA groups will keep you in the loop with any new developments of HMRC arse-ery (yes, that is a word!).

How to delight clients

This isn't as easy as you might think! As a PA I was lucky to more or less be very much appreciated by those I worked with. They considered me as the glue that held the ship together and whilst there were of course days when it was blue murder, I was very well looked after. Being a paid for service rather than as an employee is slightly different. It can feel that much harder to make an impact, especially at first and it more difficult to get feedback as it takes time for a relationship to develop when you only speak to clients weekly.

But really, delighting clients is nothing more than common sense. Do what you say you will by the agreed time, be as honest as you can if there's a problem, go the extra mile when it is appropriate*. If you cock up, own up and fix it (at your expense) and they will respect you for it.

Agree how you are going to keep in touch. I insist (because I am a demanding bitch!) that all my ongoing clients have a weekly call or Skype with me. Fortnightly, if they don't have much work on. This has two benefits for me – firstly, it builds the relationship. I get to know more about them, which means I can give them a better service. And secondly, while we're having that chat, they might or I might spot more work I can do for them. But it keeps us talking like two human beings which is a good thing in a virtual world where life can become all tasks and no human. And these calls are billable. Of course.

I want my clients to look great to their clients. For example, my voicemail message very simply says "You've reached Kathy's voicemail, please leave a message after the tone". It doesn't say anything about my business name. Why? Well, imagine one of my clients, let's call him Bob. One of his clients calls to talk to me about a meeting. They've never heard of my business name. All they know is that I look after Bob, it says so on my emails and they might think that is full-time, part-time, whatever - none of their business. But what I want for Bob is the illusion that he has dedicated support. It makes his business look bigger and better. If I start listing either my business name or all the companies I work for on my voicemail, you have a confused contact and Bob doesn't look so good any more. I want my clients to look great!

Communication is often the thing that drives clients nuts. They shouldn't be chasing you for stuff, you should always give them the information before they need to ask. And, your comms should work with their style. I have one client who utterly hates phone calls. They are torture to him. It transpired after a bit of probing that he can't bear small talk and just wants any communication to be done, fast. Catch up meetings for me, normally an hour or so, he'll be done in twenty-five minutes, I nearly scalded my mouth I drank a tea that fast. He moves at speed so I had to adjust my style to match his needs. There might come a point where that doesn't suit me or my business but for now, I can work with that. Long-term, he may be not my ideal client. Not that I need to have long rambling chats, far from it, but I do need to feel I have some kind of relationship with clients – that's where I work best - and that's really hard when it's purely operational and over in two minutes. Again, niche. Is he my ideal client personality-wise – no. Some more high tech clients may communicate best online, over message or Slack or a task management system. Everyone is different. Some you can bring around to your preferred method (or at least stop them texting, Facebook messaging, Skype messaging AND What'sApping because that's a sure way to lose your marbles) and others you won't. Then it is down to how much it gets on your tits really!

The real way I add value to my clients is a bit less tangible but once you are running your own business you totally get it. A client said to me, "I am paying you to be my friend". I nearly cried. Poor lamb, has he no friends? But I know exactly what he means. When you run your own business, even if you have staff, work is a lonely place. Partners, family and friends are interested up to a point, but they will soon get bored if they listen to the minutiae of each day. Having someone, even part time, on the team, on your side, interested and committed to your business is a huge moral support. That person can be with you through the ups and downs, suggest things, help drive the business on and be your very own cheerleader. If you can build that kind of relationship with a client, then they won't want to let you go.

This does not mean working for free! For starters, unless you state in your invoice "X hours not charged" how the hell do they even know to be grateful? Also, they will just expect you henceforth to be a magician and do four hours work in two hours and when you do the task again they'll wonder why the hell it took you twice as long as before. Record all time! Even if you decide not to bill for it. And really, in my mind, the only time you don't bill for something is if you are learning some new software (and it has to be in your interests to learn it, if only your client uses it then I say charge!) or if you make a mistake in which case don't charge for fixing it, obviously!

PA TO VA – HOW IT FEELS AND WHAT TO EXPECT

Experience

People become VAs from all sorts of backgrounds and with all sorts of experience. Particularly for those that have a specialist skill, being a VA is a good route to market. But there are some areas of experience which will make the transition easier than others. I won't say I found it easy. Not at all and I was probably the closest thing to a VA without actually being one than most people; I already worked at home, I had two jobs and juggled them across a week the best I could, and I was working for a sole trader and one small business. And I was still poleaxed when I started! So, depending on where you are at and your experience to date, you may find this harder than other people.

Small businesses work very differently to big corporates. They have a different mindset. If you have experience of working for a business of under twenty people that will really help you in your own business and to understand your clients. There aren't departments you can call in to fix things, the cash flow is totally key and the non-payment of just one invoice can really cause a huge issue. Usually, there's no such thing as a job description – everyone just mucks in.

The other thing that will help you is having had multiple bosses. Being used to juggling is very helpful. Also, working for an agency or somewhere that manages multiple clients or projects is handy. None of this is to say that you shouldn't set up as a VA, but bear in mind if you left university and spent the next twenty years working for a global bank, you WILL find this a total shock to the system. You might as well know that from the outset.

The other thing to bear in mind is that in the corporate world, technology is totally different. I used to work for a technology firm and I've learnt more since setting up on my own than I did there. Running your own VA business will involve way more IT and technical skill than normal people pick up in corporate life. And clients will not only expect you to know how to use these things, they will expect you to advise them on selecting their new CRM or the best company for VOIP calls or system for hosting a Webinar. This shouldn't stop you, but if you think this may be a weakness, crash course it! As a VA who now takes on associates who are normally newer to the business than me, nothing screams "hopeless newbie" like the moment they confess that they can't work Skype since they moved laptops or they haven't got Outlook on their PC or they don't know how to download Dropbox onto their system so they can use it in file explorer. If any of those items sounded like Chinese, you're in for shock. These are basics – I am nothing like a techie VA. I manage something like seven email addresses, three different Dropbox accounts and my own Office 365 and One Drive. And Skype (despite Microsoft's best efforts to bollocks it up with Skype for Business, bastards) and four or so Gmail calendars. The clients are going to expect you to get set up (quickly!) and when you start work with a new client they are going to expect you to take the lead on getting set up with their IT. There's mostly no such thing as an IT department. You will have to learn and learn fast! Which is easy enough if you are that way inclined but if you know technology is a challenge for you, this might make your life really tricky.

Mindset

People can find the switch from employee to business owner a challenge. As PAs, we are used to being given instructions and then getting on with the work. I wouldn't say PAs are at the bottom of the ladder, far from it, but your boss tells you what to do and you do it by and large. It is therefore quite weird for us to suddenly be an independent supplier. Especially as we're often doing a similar role and doing tasks for our clients.

Once you are set up as a VA, you have to get your head around being the boss. Not the boss of your client, your client is your client and as with any service provider, you do your best to give your client what they need. But, they aren't your boss. You get to negotiate what you want that relationship to look like, how much it is going to cost and ways of working. You couldn't do this as an employee – you're given a job description and you get on with it, adding your own flourishes as appropriate! You have much more control than you do as an employee, but only if you start as you mean to go on. That means setting some ground rules for your clients and some boundaries for yourself. Who do you want to work with? Got a dud client? You can fire them! This is now your business and you are the business owner so you decide what you want that to look like. You can set your own working hours, give yourself the day off, or you can be the whip-cracking boss from hell to yourself and work yourself into an early grave. Chances are, real life will be a blend of the two. However, should you realise that you are the worst boss to yourself you have ever had, a rethink is surely in order?

There's a thing called Imposter Syndrome. This can come and bite us all on the arse at any given moment and the thought process usually goes "who am I to……" fill in the blanks as appropriate. Who am I to start a business? Who am I to give a talk on social media? Who am I to tell someone else what to do? Who am I to mentor anyone? And so on. You get the gist. It's the heebie jeebies of suddenly losing all confidence in your abilities. And it happens to almost everyone at some point. When I first set up, I couldn't even say the words "Hello, I'm Kathy and I am a Virtual Assistant", I just felt like a total fraud. Now, I barely bat an eyelid about standing up in front of 60 people and saying it, and describing it in detail and telling them how I make my clients' lives better.

Comfort zones

There will always be something terrifying to do in your own business. At first, it'll be doing it or saying it, you'll just leap that hurdle and the next thing will come up. Or it'll be your first sales meeting or your first networking meeting. Sending your first invoice or dealing with your first associate. There doesn't really ever seem to be an end to the scary shit. It just keeps coming at you. If you are the kind of person who likes to get all squishy into a comfort zone, this is going to kill you. Because if you want your business to grow, you have to grow and that means you keep pushing yourself. That might be learning a new bit of software or standing up in front of a room full of people giving a speech (I did that! I had previously been so utterly horrified by the idea I did genuinely consider throwing a sickie at my brother's wedding so I didn't have to do a reading. Last week I did a ten-minute presentation in front of forty people and I fully expect it won't be too long before I'm up to half an hour).

Also, I have a confession to make.

I hate all my clients.

Or at least have hated them at some point.

They are remarkable, intelligent and kind people to man (and woman) but I do have a problem with them all. For the first three to six months of working with any new client I loathe it. It doesn't matter how nice they are.

Why? Well, because they are new! And I have to learn new ways of working and get to grips with their business, their systems, new software potentially and all their preferences on how they like to work. And with a few exceptions, I find that ludicrously stressful.

During the early months of every new working relationship, I go through the following stages:

Confirmed new client. Delight and excitement. OMG I have a new client!

This is amazing. I love them. I can't wait to start.

Handover day. I am wetting my knickers with excitement and a little trepidation. Full of ideas on how I can be a totally amazing addition to this business and it's going to be the best working partnership since Stan met Laurel and first got his foot stuck in a bucket (only obviously, a lot more productive).

After handover. What have I done? I can't remember all that! I don't think I wrote everything down. I forgot to ask X and Y and will have to ask and then they will think I'm a complete cockwomble.

And then basically repeat for months:

-Have I done that right?
-Oh shit, I don't have the login for that. I'll need to ask, they'll think I'm incompetent
-Fret, worry, panic to the point where I will actually make a silly mistake
-Apologise. A lot. Blow it all out of proportion and assume that if they don't fire me I definitely can't cope with working with them and need to let them go. Or throw myself on a pyre by way of retribution, you know, a small act of contrition
-All settles down until the next moment of doubt
-Repeat.

Depending on how complex the work is, this cycle can go on for months. It is exhausting. Being a VA is like being a temp every day. And yet you need to act confident and competent. This is the challenge of being a VA because clients will come and go pretty regularly. You're no sooner in your comfort zone than something will throw you out again. And you have to have the resilience to deal with that.

SOMETIMES IT'S A BITCH

Sometimes, being your own boss sucks. It just does. Most of the time it doesn't but there are days when you just want to say, "bollocks to this" and go work on a checkout in Tesco. Then you remember all the really annoying people and their even more annoying screeching children in Tesco and backtrack wildly. But you could. It could push you that far.

The challenge of finding and managing your own work is a biggie in the stress stakes. One day, a VA will wake up and say, "I have the perfect amount of work to complete this week in the allotted time and it is going to pay me handsomely". You will then see Peppa Pig and her porcine buddies flitting across the sky in feather boas giving her the finger.

You've already read the section about the agony that is billing by the hour and the fact that I now factor in time to obsess, fret and worry about my billable hours (seriously, if I'm going to do it, it might as well be planned into my day as "non-billable planning"!). But you just think you are about there, it's sort of balanced and you have a fair idea what is coming in when and, wallop, a client leaves. So, you have a hole to fill. You think you've filled it, you're good to go and, wallop, hot lead goes away.

And this is the reality of freelance life. You can never rest on your laurels and assume that work will be forthcoming. Sometimes it is. Sometimes the universe just casually spits clients at you and you barely have to lift a finger to make that happen. More often than not though, it's harder work than that and new work is the result of hours and hours of networking, getting to know people and drinking shit coffee at 7am.

So that's the roller coaster of freelance life hours. It's annoying. But it is what it is. Last week I was still working at 9pm two nights in a row because I had so much on. It goes up. It goes down. Up. Down. C'est la vie.

But as well as client work (or lack thereof) there are SO many things that can conspire to make you have a crap day and you are best to know about these upfront.

- Prospective clients that fully expected you were going to charge them £10 an hour.
- Prospective clients that dick you about and waste your time. (Or lie to you! I had a man contact me about some VA support. When I turned up at the meeting (driving an hour each way!) he tried to recruit me as a Juice Plus sales person. What. The. Actual. Fuck. If that happened now I'm older, wiser and a LOT more jaded I swear I'd have his balls off with a hole punch - how very fucking dare you?).
- If you're ill and you either have to work anyway in your half dead state or factor in not getting paid for a day.
- If your technology fails and you waste a load of time, money and effort just trying to get yourself back to a place where you CAN work. By which time you're so knackered and cross you might as well just have a bottle of wine anyway.
- If you don't get picked for a job.
- If you DO get picked for a job you've invested time in winning and it transpires to be an hour of bloody data entry (after a four-hour sales process).

So, if you are making the move to freelancing you have to be fairly robust. You have to be able to roll with the punches (hole or otherwise) and you have to get yourself some decent support. There is a whole section on support because it is so key.

Values

One of the truly fabulous things about running your own business is that you can have your own set of values. A company I worked for many years ago used to do many a workshop on this, mine are a bit more cobbled together. In fact, I knew I had them but until writing this section I'd never even written them down! They are in my brain, or perhaps, more importantly, they are in my gut.

Gut feelings are so important. If something doesn't feel right, it probably isn't (or, it could be evil PMT fucking with your head, in which case, wait a few days before making any big decisions just in case and certainly don't quit anything or get a haircut!) and you need to listen to why that might be.

So, my business values are apparently:

- I do whatever is in the best interest of the client / prospect
  - So this means, if a prospect comes to me for work and I can see a way they could get it done better or cheaper elsewhere, I tell them – even if I lose the job. If I am not right for the client at any point, I will let them go or find them someone else, again, even if that means I lose the work. If I can find ways of getting things done better, faster, cheaper I do them, even if that reduces my hours or eliminates me entirely.
- I treat others as I want to be treated
  - Pretty obviously really. Don't screw people over, offer help where you can to those who need it and don't be a (total) bitch.
  - There is also something undefined about being prepared to pay for effort and expertise, valuing others time, as I expect others to value my time.
- Where it can be done, I buy local
  - Supporting other small UK businesses where possible.
- I champion UK VAs as an industry and am part of raising standards

and good business practice.

I think that's all I have. I may have to stick them on the wall right now!

CLIENTS

Gut feelings

One thing to think about when looking for clients is …. Do you actually want them? It's tempting to just say yes to everything but be warned! Not every client is a good client. Some are more trouble than they are worth. I've been relatively lucky to date but have heard some horror stories. This is my business. I am not employed any more. And do you know what this means? This means I only work with people I want to work with.

I will say that again.

I only work with people I want to work with.

I have "fired" a client because after three weeks I was losing my mind and I didn't want to work with them anymore. Now, what I should have done was listen to my initial gut feeling that this was a seriously loopy bunch of people and they were going to be a right pain in the arse. Because guess what? They were! They were lovely human beings but their business model was (to me) like a bunch of vomit in a bowl swirling around at top speed. I don't love that; ambiguity, flakiness and chaos aren't good for me. I should never have said yes in the first place, I should have heard the alarm bells ringing.

Since that, I am much better at listening to my gut. This all sounds very good BUT (and this is where I struggle) when I have PMT I hate bloody everybody. So how do I know that this person isn't right for me or if really, if I met Mother Theresa and the Dalai Lama today to work on their new JV they wouldn't also completely get on my tits? It's a bastard. Days like that I long to be a man, I really do.

So, if I know I don't have swarms of hormones that might mean I need to be more logical, less emotional and do my best not to think everyone is a total git, I try and go with my gut. I'm sure there are many more types of clients to avoid like the plague, but here's a few I have met and escaped from or heard about from others.

Penny Pinching

Everyone loves a bargain. Of course, they do. But beware penny pinching behaviour because it will make life awkward.

These types quite often self-filter I find. They get in touch, we talk, I give them prices, they run away. Job done. If I have suspicions, then I give them higher prices – you can always negotiate down but getting prices back up is a real challenge. It's usually not the ones that can't afford it that are the problem, it's the ones that can afford it but just have an innate need to be as tight as a nun's knicker elastic for the sake of it.

I had one client (briefly!) and I did some onsite work for him. He had me send back a windscreen wiper blade because in the time it took to arrive he'd changed his car. This chap lived in a very nice part of London, car number one was a BMW, car number two an Audi. The windscreen wipers cost about £12. Me, I'd just chuck them if no one else could use them. He had me call the garage, arrange to post them back, actually post them back, then chase for a credit note. It must have cost him more than £12 in billed time and postage to have me do it. What on earth is the point? This is the kind of thing that if it hadn't been early on in my adventures I would have been waving red flags "tight bastard alert, run". I didn't, I assumed he was a total plonker of course. But it didn't raise alarms. It certainly would now. It is penny pinching behaviour to a ridiculous degree. Because it isn't about the £12, I don't like waste or losing money either, it's the total inability to look at the bigger picture.

The same with clients who regularly question how long it takes you to do things. If you are going to spend your life agonising over three minutes on a timesheet you are probably not right for me. I am a very fast worker so if I am questioned (and it's very rare) I know there's an issue. Could I do things faster? Maybe. Could I do it faster and have it at a fabulous standard? No, not always. Don't get me wrong, on certain jobs it is helpful to have a time estimate or a maximum because some tasks you could carry on with forever, especially research. In those moments, it's worth having a conversation along the lines of "Shall I do half an hour and let you know where I'm at?" or "Can you spend no more than an hour on this?" But the minutiae of each task, no no no! You are paying me to think, I would hope. How can I think if I'm wellying along at a million miles an hour?

For me this is a two-pronged annoyance and it kind of bashes against my values in an unhelpful way. Firstly, if you take on a supplier you pay for the best you can afford. If you want cheap, go cheap, but know that the standard might be a bit dubious. If you decide to buy quality, then pay for it. Would you take a Mulberry handbag up to the cashier and start haggling to get it at £50? No? Well some of these folks might – this is that type. They can't help themselves. Not that I am a Mulberry handbag, but neither am I a knock-off that is being flogged on eBay for £20. I'm perhaps a Radley bag? It doesn't matter. I'm just saying, you get what you pay for. You commit to paying for what you agreed. If you want more of it, you still have to pay. Ask for a discount if you are buying twenty handbags, maybe. But not for one. Or that thing where you ask for a free keyring or something. It annoys me. I can't work with people like that. Not only as a supplier to them, but it is a total nightmare dealing with their suppliers as they will expect you to behave the same way to get free stuff, cheap stuff and generally stretch the boundaries of working relationships and common courtesy to their limits. And they will be the first to complain when whatever it is they have scrounged on the cheap or for free isn't up to standard. Or worse, make you do it. Beware of those always after something for nothing!

And there is the second issue of trust. Clients I work with I want the kind of relationship where they trust me. By saying "did it really take that long" that is heading towards "I don't believe you". In these days of electronic time recording, I am not guessing, I am clicking in and out. If it has taken wildly longer than expected then there will almost certainly have been conversations about it, but that rarely happens. The iron triangle of project management is fast, good and cheap. By all accounts you can pick two of the three but three is unattainable. Bear this in mind when talking to penny pinchers.

The 80/20 lot

I just don't know what else to call these people. They are people who will spend 80% of the time talking to you about work, getting you to meetings, coffees, having you send proposals, negotiating on email – and the work itself takes about ten minutes. So, you are 80% non-billable 20 % billable.

I have had clients ask me to three meetings before they have bought anything. Remembering that I am virtual, this is a royal pain in the arse. It is even more of a royal pain in the arse when the amount of time they have actually used my services for is less than the time I have spent driving to and from meetings, never mind the meetings themselves.

A slow burn sale isn't always a bad thing (and a quick one sometimes can be very bad, let me tell you!) but in my experience, ones that begin this way tend to carry on this way. They don't commit to a decent number of hours, it'll be a pissy amount. Sometimes they are also "onsite or die" types (see later) and they then don't see anything done outside of their building as work and therefore as billable. Talking about the work is billable. But you do have to have actually started which is where this lot fail spectacularly.

What is particularly annoying about these folks is that they assume that you should be delighted to do this work. That you should see this ninety minutes every now and then as a huge favour. Er, no! I have jobs of twenty hours a month that took ten minutes to sell. This took ten hours to sell and it'll be three years before I actually make back my cost of sale. And you want a discount? Erm, let me think. Er, no.

All clients are important, all work is important but those that value my time are more important and will always get priority. Always.

Broom up arse syndrome

Happily, I have never managed to have one of these as a client, they don't get that far after you have a sensible conversation with them. But here is how that conversation usually goes:

"So, what kind of work do you need a VA to be doing for you?"
"Well, I want my invoices doing, and receipts. And reconciliation. And chasing late payers."
"OK, totally doable."
"And then I need meetings booked, travel and hotel arrangements made for my ten trips overseas every year"
"Good"
"And I'll want you to be first point of contact for any clients that get in touch."
"And what kind of response time is there on that?"
"Oh, four hours tops. And then I'll want all my meeting notes typed up, my social media posts done, blogs written and responses done on any Twitter comments. I run events quarterly that all need organising, and a weekly webinar so I want that done and I have a regular newsletter that needs writing."
"That all sounds fine. It is quite a large amount of work potentially"
"Well, I only have budget for ten hours a month."

And that right there is your problem! All this work is totally doable but all of that, in ten hours? Dream on. Naturally, that isn't what I say…

"That number of hours is unlikely to be able to cover all those areas. I suggest, as a starting point, we select the ones that are most important. As an example, I do another client's invoicing, reconciliation, payment chasing and some meeting arrangements and that takes me between six and eight hours a month. Which areas do you most want to outsource?"

And it is usually at this point that they realise that what they need is someone full-time or to re-evaluate what they can get done. Often, they really think that they can have their whole life, business and personal, sorted for £200 a month, we're good but we aren't that good! They often also don't realise that some VAs specialise and some are generalist. But the likelihood of getting someone who is brilliant at everything is pretty low. You want a book-keeper, website builder, CRM manager, marketing strategist, social media strategist, oh and some admin. Which isn't to say that VAs can't outsource some things but, really, would you expect one person to be brilliant at everything? What they think a VA is, is a fulltime employee (or three!) you only have pay for a few hours. Which leads us neatly to:

Always on 'Arry

One of the most challenging aspects of being a VA for me is managing client's expectations on time. If you are paying me for ten hours a month, you can't realistically expect me to be at my desk waiting for your call for forty hours a week. It's not logical. You pay me for ten hours, I'll maybe check your emails twice a day and chunk time to do your work twice a week. I cannot drop everything to respond to an email within ten minutes. I have meetings, other client work, onsite work and so on. If you want someone at your beck and call then there's a word for that – employee. Full-time employee in fact. And even they take lunch breaks, holidays and go and pee! I often have this conversation with new clients and once you explain it, they totally get it. But they didn't get it before it was spelt out, which was a learning for me – they need educating. And that is totally fine. I knew naff all about how being a VA works, why on earth should I expect anyone else to be psychic? I'll explain it during an onboarding conversation (see later) and then everyone knows where they are at.

Your Always On 'Arry types will fully expect you to be available to reply at all times because in their head you are their PA, never mind the fact that they are only paying you for a fraction of that time. This is why I never ever do call handling – I don't want to be trapped and waiting.

What they don't realise is that checking emails, answering calls takes time. If you are only paying me for ten hours a month, I do not sit at my desk waiting for something to come in for you so I can do it. I have to manage and plan my time to fit everyone in and you might get a slot every other day for me to check in and do what is needed. What I don't do is work on your stuff all the time. Because I only have ten hours a month to play with. If you send me (or CC me on) a hundred emails a day, they are going to take time to read. It is entirely possible that I might spend six of those ten hours reading a lot of emails. Leaving only four hours to do some actual work. And if these emails (or in some cases, emails, WhatsApps, Facebook messages, texts AND Skype messages!) come at me at all hours I am pretty soon going to have no time left of your ten-hour block. And as a VA I am not checking emails all day every day. Even if I keep a glance on them, I may not be able to action them immediately ("Can you cancel the meeting at 2pm? We're engrossed in something" It now being 1pm and I am onsite with a different client – no, not doable. If you want that level of cover, you'll be needing a fulltime employee, who is hopefully not on a lunchbreak at that moment or that won't work either).

Some businesses work funny hours and some may even have multiple VAs to cover that (for example, having a USA based VA to cover UK evenings) but clients must respect that I don't work twenty-four hours a day. I had a text (or an email, can't remember) from a newish client at 7.45 on a Friday evening with no apology, asking if I could book a car to pick him up the next morning. Er, no! Have some respect. Either ask me earlier or do it yourself. As it was, the other VA he'd also emailed and I both studiously ignored the email until Monday morning (without even a conversation! Psychic twins of "are you having a laugh?"). Sure enough, he did it himself. It took no more time than emailing us - that's prize-winning knob behaviour right there. And although it does irritate me, I am trying to educate by using behaviourism*.

So, behaviourism - rewarding good behaviour and ignoring or punishing the bad (electric shocking clients is most probably illegal). I have a friend who is a very high level PA and she has a sort of behaviourist system. Most people prioritise tasks by urgency, type, whatever. She prioritises by whether the person that gave it to her is an arsehole or not. If you have ever pissed this woman off, your task might well be so far down her metaphorical in-tray it won't see the light of day until her retirement. This is exactly behaviourism in action. Also known as "Don't piss off the PA, your life won't be worth living". Their jobs don't get done, their meetings with her boss are always at shitty times and they probably have to beg for those shitty slots four times. Things may even be lost, or never done, messages mysteriously not passed on, emails disappeared. And she'll be desperately pleasant about it and make it seem very reasonable whilst being totally unhelpful. Those people who are polite, respectful and generally pleasant to work with think she's the best, most efficient PA in the universe and a total honey. Which she is... if you treat her right. I assume now that in the company induction there is some kind of introduction to this. But there shouldn't need to be if everyone treated each other with respect.

So, your man with his car, ignore. Everything out of hours, studiously ignore. I am not meant to be at my desk therefore I haven't read it. In fact, although I do quite often do work out of hours, because I know it is very annoying to get emails at night, I will put a delay on any emails I send with Boomerang so they don't appear until a reasonable time.

The problem with us VAs is that we are a helpful bunch. So, we say "yes", a lot more than we should. Saying no is challenging but I am training myself to do it more.

Friday afternoon at 5pm "can this letter I am just sending go out today? Or tomorrow?"
My instinct is to go "of course, I'll do that"
My brain is saying "Fuck off! I'm four and a half minutes away from a very large glass of wine and tomorrow is Saturday and I'm screwed if I'm doing it then in between having a life and mowing the lawn. The last thing I want to do is queue in the bloody post office for thirty minutes with the great unwashed."

What I should say is "I can get that out for you Monday". It's not a no. It's not unreasonable. What usually happens, because I am pathetic, is that I will make up a load of bollocks about how I am away all weekend ("literally just running out the door now") and end up at some point hiding in Tesco when I run into said client down the frozen food aisle... It's not grown up enough. I really must try harder.

And, on behaviourism, by the same token, when I get an email that says "next week / month, I have X on and will need some extra time, can you save me some?" I am very effusive in my thanks for their impressive organisation and foresight because it makes my life easier. Rewarding good behaviour.

And I'm not a bitch (hard to tell I know). In a crisis, out of hours I will help if it's a one-off thing. My clients very very rarely (now I've culled some of those I didn't much gel with!) ask for things out of hours. So, on the rare occasion there is an issue I will bust a gut to help. If it's not taken for granted, that's fine. It's the assumption that gets on my wick.

Behaviourism. Actual psychology stuff. Proper sensible books are strongly advised before putting this into practice. Google Pavlov's dog for a quick and dirty idea of the basics.

Onsite or die

How can work possibly be done if I can't see it? Hmmmm. I wonder. I have a special magic thing called "broadband" that enables me to connect with people wherever I am. And I have little computer and a desk. And a chair. Everything I need to do work (which, incidentally is a lot better set up than a lot of these clients who insist I schlep out to them! You would not BELIEVE some of the places I've worked).

Some clients need me to be onsite. They do. The work is paper, there's lots of it, it needs putting into places with more paper that they also have. That's fair and sensible enough. There is also an element of working together, which I love and totally get and think is very valuable. Sometimes even "working together" on separate things can be a good thing for the client because it is earmarked time in their diary so it's protected. I do work with several clients face to face once a month and it's brilliant.

I also love working with clients at their events and workshops and so on. Again, fabulous, love to be there, bring it on.

But some clients feel the need to have you present even when there is absolutely no need whatsoever, like they can't believe you could ever manage to work without supervision. I don't know if this is a trust thing or an ego thing or just an old fashioned-ness. It's annoying if it can't be managed and properly priced but if it can be managed, it's not the worst thing for me. The nastiest moment I ever had with a client was when she refused to pay for offsite work and only pay for onsite. She was clearly a batshit-crazy cow (on many levels) but it goes to show people not understanding the concept of VAs and how time is billable. You know, all of it, not just the bits you want to pay for or personally witness...

Goldfish

Some clients forget about your existence when you aren't actually in front of them. So, although you can work remotely the chances of these people ever giving you any work offsite is slim because they are too swamped by a million things to ever do something as radical as answer an email or a ringing phone. Much less actually get in touch off their own bat (or if they do and you reply it'll be four weeks before they then respond again). Basically, if you want to work for them, you really have to be there and in their face. And book the next one while you are there because you will never hear from them between times, it's like the Bermuda Triangle. This is one frustrating thing about being virtual. If these clients were actual onsite colleagues, you'd just pester them at their desk. They never have time to ever return calls or emails or God forbid do the actual work they should be doing. All of which just turns their lives into a vicious circle of busyness and never getting things done.

What is most annoying is that these are the people who most need a VA. And preferably a VA that is going to kick some arse and get them stricter on their working methods – because working the way they do is chaotic and very likely to end up with balls dropped. Not so much one or two balls but an entire ball pool of balls dropped. BUT they can't slow down and focus for one second to even look at the bigger picture without interruptions. We have all worked with these people – they have the attention span of gnats. Think Finding Nemo "just keep swimming, just keep swimming, oh look, krill". Whatever is shiniest or most urgent gets done, unless someone interrupts with something else in which case that gets done first, regardless of whether that is a priority, because the person happened to walk in the room or ring or whatever. They are poor time managers, allowing disruptions to take over and never keeping to time on anything – meetings drag on for hours even though they clearly don't need to, hundreds of emails remain unread, deadlines pass. I saw one client fail to call a very important customer who had an issue because of various interruptions which by comparison were trivial. Despite almost incessant pestering and nagging from me and two of the team the 2pm planned call time became 3.30pm turning a mildly-irked-customer into an incandescent-with-rage-customer. That is a Goldfish for you, just swimming along, making life harder for themselves.

I don't especially love working with Goldfish (you can probably tell!). Mainly because, I am one of these people that does things when I say I will. And it pisses me off royally when others don't do the same. Or worse, when I am witness to my client's clients being left without things being done and I have no control over it, as with that call. I want my clients to succeed, I feel part of their team – and I therefore feel the failure when something goes wrong. You spend so much time chasing, nagging, reminding and basically wasting time that it isn't a fun client to have. Also, they are very bad payers usually as paying invoices falls way down their list of to dos – again, you waste time beating money out them (figuratively! I've yet to "send in the boys").

And being so bloody diabolical at managing their own time, often they have little regard for others time. Including mine. So, they won't pay attention to things like deadlines, set up, the how to of working with a VA – they will just steamroller on in their own way totally oblivious to the fact that they are actually costing you money by behaving like this. At this point being onsite is a huge advantage – if I am onsite they are paying me. If they haven't managed to sort out any work for me because they are goldfishing along, well, that's their problem for once and not mine. I've had a goldfish cost me money because I turned down some new work because she'd said she wanted fifteen hours in a month to get a project done …. And then she never managed to do what she needed to do so I could do the work. I now don't let her have retained time, she has to pay me Ad Hoc rates and if I have time she can get her work done. But I won't hold time for her again after that.

We all have days where the volume of work feels overwhelming but the more that is the case, the greater the need to take a step back, calm the fuck down and prioritise. And plan. And strategise. Which means saying no to people. And locking doors, turning off email and your phone. And if it lasts longer than a few weeks and you never ever get on top of your work mountain then clearly you need something else to happen – whatever that might be.

I'm not sure that these folks don't enjoy the chaos, the pressure. Maybe they do. If they don't then surely, they are heading for a heart attack – I feel I am some days just witnessing it, it's genuinely exhausting. After a day with a Goldfish I am usually in need of a very stiff drink. They wear me out!

It should be said as a disclaimer that not all Goldfish are permanent Goldfish. We are all capable of having Goldfish-like moments. If you have never been a Goldfish then all I can say is that either, you have never had a huge pressure of work, or you never sleep. When the volume of work is insane, it is very easy to just fire fight and get your head into a horrible place. What you need at that point is a helpful, polite and charming VA to shout "Oi, mate. You're a Goldfish". And all will be well.

Wierdos and nutters

There are some days when I think that I have "Weirdos apply here" tattooed on my forehead. It might just be me, but I do seem to attract the eccentric and barmy clients and tasks on occasion.

I was reassured by a fellow VA that I am not alone in the weirdo-magnetic stakes. I give you her tale of woe:

So ... on responding to a People Per Hour job ad three years ago - the usual slick and brilliant proposal that I tailor for every prospect - I got an immediate response from this "tech start-up entrepreneur". So, keen he was to talk, we connected on Skype and were talking within the hour -

no video - luckily (read on). All excited was I, a new client, perhaps another private client (I'd soon be able to ditch the VA company and go it alone - woo hoo!). After five minutes of talking, the tone changed from finding out about me and what I did to "is the sun shining?" to "nice, so it's hot then?" to "are you wearing shorts or a dress?", to errrrrrr! Fuck! Heavy breathing on the other end of Skype!!! HANG UP!!!!!!!! Basically, I was all excited about a new client, but this perv had other things to be excited about! Cringe!!!!!

And many people get lunatic stalkers on LinkedIn. It is genuinely tragic that in this day and age men (a minority, not all) feel it is totally appropriate to comment on a woman's appearance on a work site when she is talking about work, an expert in her work and looking for work. (I spelt that out very clearly in case there are any such men reading as I don't think they are masters of subtlety).

I blame myself for the most recent one. I put an advert in my local village newsletter, mainly to support it because it's cute and I think it's important to keep these local things going. My little ad next to the latest news and views from the WI, the vicar and the Horticultural Society's Spring update. What could possibly go wrong?!?

Mainly Albert and Vera, that's what can go wrong!

In a huge swing away from my usual B2B client base and talking to very serious corporate entities in big shiny offices, it seems I now have on the books a couple of pensioners with weird and wonderful collections of "stuff" that needs cataloguing so it can be sold. Me and my laptop rock up to be greeted with a gramophone collection, three thousand cigarette cards, fifteen hundred ornamental cats and a half hour of reminiscence about having lots of "gals" in a typing pool. Then, having knocked up a spreadsheet in two minutes flat to add the data into I had to be watched whilst typing it in, just in case I wasn't up to speed (not being a "gal from a typing pool" thank the Lord for small mercies I was born thirty years too late). This from the man who until five minutes before had no idea that such a thing as a spreadsheet actually existed!

After this torturous effort, it was back home with almost a whole seven items to enter into said spreadsheet just to check I could manage (I didn't point out that my last epic old-school data entry job was three

WHOLE A4 BOXES of business cards). Four minutes on the timesheet or something ludicrous. Again, God forbid I balls up a spreadsheet so simple even a monkey could use it. And then I get "can you send us an invoice. I've found more cards so I'm not really ready to start properly yet". Lordy. An invoice is created for less than an hour's work. Off it goes...

"What's your address for the cheque, dear?"

At this point I bang my head slowly on the desk for a moment.

It will take me longer to drive into town, park using the bastard pay-by-phone-app, walk to the bank and pay in the cheque and come home than the actual work took to complete. Not on your bloody life, this is already far too surreal for my liking. I'm not adding swearing at the pay-by-phone lady to my stresses for the grand sum of £27.50. I write back. Politely explaining that it is not 1982 and there's this magic thing calls BACS. (honestly, I was as nice as I could humanly muster).

"Ooh no dear. We don't use that do we Albert?"

Cash it is then! Sure enough, the postie delivered me £30 in crisp notes today with a letter saying, "keep the change"! I honestly still don't know whether to laugh or cry and part of me deeply hopes that when the moment of great cataloguing is nigh, I am vastly overrun with other things... Love 'em.

Super clients

So, if there are all these God-awful clients or wannbe clients, why on earth would you do this? Well, because, when you get a brilliant client it makes up for all the challenging ones. What makes a Super client?

Trust. They trust you to do a good job, be honest and let you get on with it. Not necessarily straightaway, there's always a learning curve, but in time they are happy for you to do your bit without any in depth interference.

Respect. They respect your time, your experience and you as a person. They understand that you have multiple clients and are not at their beck and call 24/7. They ask for and value your opinion.

Good personality match. By and large, I like my clients as people enough that I'd go out for a beer with them. Having a great working relationship doesn't mean we have to socialise, we don't, but we are friendly enough that we could.

Working with a Super client feels good. It's satisfying, you can have open conversations and feel confident making suggestions to improve their business. It's like you really are part of a team. I know I'm in a good place with a client when they call me to tell me about their business. Not because I need to do anything but because they either value me as a sounding board or they know that I will want to know about a success or an issue. By this point, they get that I am on their team and I actually care. That's when I know I'm with the right client for me. Their business is important to me as are they – not in a "the client is always important" way but in a genuine, "I care" way.

But getting on well isn't enough on its own. The work has to be right as well. The work for a Super client can vary but for me it allows me to make a difference and usually it's not just admin. Obviously, there is admin, in most jobs, but this will typically be a bit more than that. Parts of it will certainly allow me some independence and responsibility.

So, who are these people? They will be different for everyone of course, but for me, they are usually one man or woman bands. They tend to work business to business so their clients are other businesses. They are smart and have strong personalities. They realise there is more to life than work so they typically aren't entrepreneurs working a hundred and twenty hours a week. But that's me. It took me a long time to work out who my Super client is and it isn't fool proof.

I now keep on my wall a list of the qualities of my preferred clients. This gives me an idea when I am doing my marketing who I should be targeting. It also makes me think before I say yes to random things. This list isn't really a list of professions, more who people are as people and how their businesses run. Naturally, I have clients on my books that don't really fit this exact mould as we looked at in the Niche section, but

I enjoy working with them and they work despite not really fitting the ideal client brief. That's OK! It's not a do or die thing, more a where I want to be thing. Plus, there might be the most amazing person about to rock up into my life, I'm not going to say no simply because of a list! The most important thing to me is respect and if my clients are respectful (value my time, pay invoices in a timely manner, want to commit to the relationship) then they are Super clients and I will love working with them.

Sales – How does one find these client things then?

Congratulations, you are now self-employed and entirely responsible for finding your own work. Consider yourself the newly appointed Head of Sales, or Sales Director, if you prefer. From this point on, as well as actually doing the work, you will also need to spend a considerable amount of time finding work to do. This is the one area which makes people give up. Either because for some reason they didn't see this coming, or they didn't realise how hard it would be, or they just can't find enough work to keep them afloat.

Typically, it takes time to find a new client. It is a lot of seed-sowing and then eventually, things come good. Take networking, many people (and I was one!), think that networking is about who is actually in the room and whether they might be clients. It isn't! Networking is about getting to know the people in the room, having them get to know (and hopefully like!) you and then months down the line when they talk to someone they know who has a need, with luck, you will spring to mind and they will hunt out your business card. It's a slow burn. Although, flukes happen and one morning I rocked up to a BNI meeting only to meet another visitor and he became a client for a year. But that's rare. I know this now. This was my first "proper" networking meeting and I genuinely thought that they would all go like this and I'd have a full portfolio of clients in a fortnight. Sadly not.

My first clients came from my network or my extended network of contacts. LinkedIn is just amazing for this. After I set up on my own, various people who knew me as a PA made contact once they saw what I was now doing. I was lucky enough to have one consultant I worked with, email his entire network and tell them that if they ever needed a VA they'd best call me, what a sweetie. And in time, this did lead to one client who is still on my books today.

Since then, clients have come from recommendations, from networking groups I have been a part of, via my old jobs, from a random conversation on Facebook, from an ad in my local village newsletter (I don't know who was more surprised, me or the editor!) and, most obscurely, my dog walking group! There are opportunities everywhere and although there are times when you feel you have no new prospects on the horizon, that can change in a heartbeat.

Of course, I didn't rely on getting clients by luck. When I first set up, I networked my arse off. If there was an opening of an envelope, I was at it with a big smile and a pile of business cards.

Another way to find work and learn at the same time is to take on associate work for other, longer established VAs but you still have to find that work. See the separate chapter on working as an Associate.

So, here is my run down on where to find those elusive clients.

Online work sites

One way that some VAs get work is by using online sites – for example, People per Hour, Upwork, Elance and Fiverr and many more. I haven't used them myself so I can't give a definitive answer on it but they are task based by and large, rather than relationship based. These sites are about competing on price and if you are competing against US or Far East VAs then you are going to be (I hope!) a lot more expensive. A quick search on People per Hour shows UK Virtual Assistants charging as little as £7 per hour. That's less than the UK living wage for an employee. they'd make more money stacking shelves AND they'd get holiday pay!

If you wanted to be Siri when you grew up, fill your boots and sign up. Personally, I like clients who want to talk to me rather than to a robotic task functioning creature. I had a client (A Penny Pincher, naturally) who wanted his books done and had me post the task on a site for bids. It's just a task market and I am more of a people girl so I leave it well alone. In my quick search, I also saw that people charge $5 to video themselves getting custard pies thrown in their face or to make a prank call to anyone of your choosing. It was a wormhole of weirdness that I was sucked into for far too long, wow. What people will do for $5!

However, having said all that, if you have a very niche skill that not many others have it might work to get to a wider audience or to get some work under your belt when you first set up. For me, because I am such a generalist, I don't use them.

Social media, marketing and virtual networking

This is where most VAs do get their work from. But it is a hard slog! It is all about getting to know people so that if someone is looking for a VA you will get the nod. This is where having a niche helps. Are you to go to girl for anything medical? A whizz on Canva? Once people know that, they'll start recommending you.

What is key is knowing where online your ideal client spends time. Or, if they don't, then you don't want to be spending hours and hours online – get into the real world! Typically, LinkedIn is the business site but Facebook and Twitter are becoming increasingly great places for referrals. The best thing to do is to get some training if you're clueless. It'll help you with your business and you will then have more insight if a client asks you to do social media work for them.

As with almost every aspect of being a VA, there are some excellent Facebook groups where you can go and soak up loads of experience. VAs are typically very generous with their knowledge. However, don't be a knob and get in a group and ask 14 questions a day – firstly, people will help but that's taking the piss. They all have actual client work to do and they will quickly start calling you "that bloody annoying one who asks all the questions". Secondly, if you are spending your entire time asking questions about every last bloody thing it almost certainly means you aren't just getting on with it. Needing to know everything 100% before you do it is not going to stand you in good stead as a freelancer. Also, lots of questions will already have been answered and a quick search of the page would give you what you need. Asking the same question as sixteen other people makes you look needy or worst case, stupid! It's like the people who ask, "what time do I need to get a train to get to London at nine?" There's this magic thing called Google…

Remember too that online networking is a bit like online dating. I assume that you have half a brain but scammers are getting more devious by the day. Clearly don't send bank details or passwords to people. Be highly suspicious of anyone offering a "job" if you do an interview or complete a test task. In this case, do ask other VAs if you have a sniff of suspicion. Some people aren't evil, just stupid and that's life. Have some basics in place – a contract, agreed rates etc. and do a bit of research to make sure your "client" is who they say they are. It goes without saying that by and large most people who claim to be a Nigerian Prince or similar, aren't.

Real world networking

Ah, networking. This is the thing that I do to find new clients. Well, mostly. People in jobs talk about networking with their peers and getting known, rocking up to an industry dinner with some dull old gits and kicking about at a seminar for half a day to blag some free notebooks. Their version is like a nice aquarium with some pretty clown fish and a bit of coral, the company pays and at worst it's a bit dull and is keeping you from doing some actual work (which may be a good or bad thing!).

As a self-employed person networking is not like that at all. Our version is like being a guppy hurled into the shark pool at Seaworld AND you have to bloody pay for it. AND you aren't earning any money while you're there. That isn't to say it's awful. It's a culture shock is what it is. I don't mind them now but God, when I first started I was like a deer in headlights – I'd have been less freaked out standing up at an AA meeting. Face to face networking is seen as scary to the point where lots of VAs never even do it! But if it doesn't kill you it makes you stronger in my book. I've been to a few different types of networking and below are my experiences of them. I know people that love the ones I hate and loathe the ones I love. It's a very personal thing. For me, it has to a) bring me business AND b) not make me want to stick free hotel pens in my eyes. Others are happy just with option A and have much stronger stomachs for early mornings and American cheerleading bollocks. Until you try, you will never know. There's one big networking organisation I still haven't made it to yet for one reason or another but by and large I'll try anything...

This is my run down on all types.

Local Random Groups
These have proved to be my favourite so far. I am insanely lucky in that I was introduced to one such group even before I began my business and it is everything I like! It's run as a not-for-profit (so any surplus goes into a pot and we have a big Christmas piss up!). It's small enough that we can sit around one table and it is very much the same people every week. This is brilliant in that you get to understand what everyone does really well and build up trust and productive relationships. It is also perfect as a "I've got this challenge, what does everyone think I should do?" forum and for that alone it's invaluable. It is also cheap because it isn't anyone's company which most networking businesses are – most are there to make a profit. I suppose the only downside of it is that it isn't that big (although we don't really want it to be!) so the opportunities for meeting new people are limited. But that is very minor when I consider the plus sides. I enjoy it, I really like the people and the food is good. It's only twice a month, no one beats you up if you can't make it and everyone genuinely tries to help each other – with advice, introductions or just moral support! For me, if everyone who started a business had access to a group like this it would be amazing.

All of us in this group are looking for other similar groups because it is so fab and have yet to find one quite the same. This group is very different as it isn't owned by anyone. Normally, running a networking group is quite a bit of work (you can run a franchise or set up your own) and so the person doing it expects to be rewarded for their effort. This might be free membership, a percentage of take or whatever, but something. Our wonderful little group splits the effort (and actually, it isn't much because we don't want to grow so there isn't any marketing or selling to do!) and someone does the money, someone gets the food pre-order, someone chairs (and that isn't very taxing) and then someone organises events every so often. And roles rotate when someone has had enough! Now if you compare that effort to a networking group that I did some paid work for – wow, no comparison.

There is also a very informal thing that I am loving organised by some working mums in my local town. A few neighbours got together over a few glasses of wine (honestly, the best ideas are formed this way as far as I can tell – I bet Archimedes was sat in his bath with a fine vintage when he sussed out displacement) and thought to themselves "I bet there are lots of women in this town that are very smart and do lots of interesting things. Shall we get them all together?" And an idea was born. It is in its infancy and it is a mix of employed and self-employed people so not hugely my target market but it kind of is. Because the rule of networking is always – it isn't who is in the room, it's who they know. Well that's one rule that official people say, I have loads more myself (see – Rules of Networking for more). But I'm a sociable kind of girl, it's one night a month (on a night I can actually make for once!), it's really interesting meeting a huge mix of people and there's wine. What's not to like? Again, there's no profit involved just a cool group of three (I think) women (all in corporate jobs and very happy FYI) who decided that it would be a shit hot idea to meet some local women in a networky / not networky kind of way. Good on them.

Local Business Initiatives
In most areas, the local council will have a set of people who are there to help small businesses. I am on the border of two counties so do tart about a bit between the two quite shamelessly. The support where I am ranges from a "hub" where membership (free) means you can get a free meeting room, working area and Wi-Fi, to local networking events of various sorts and awards and all sorts. It would be a fulltime job just to work out what they can and do provide. But if you look, there is a lot of support. It's tricky to find but this lot do offer networking in many different ways at many different cost levels. I have done a few (on my guilt list to do more it really is) but usually the cost is somewhere between free and not that expensive. For me, the downside is that they are normally smack in the middle of the day which challenges my billable hours panic levels...

There are loads of networking opportunities when you start looking for them. When I was newly set up I went to everything, and I mean everything. Networking can take many forms, I often go to award launches or Expos. They want people in the room, I want to meet people. Lovely job.

The BIG one – BNI

This is the most well-known of the for-profit companies. It started in the USA and is now pretty much everywhere. Some people have built entire businesses just going to this one group. Personally, I don't love it. I don't have the intense loathing of it that many people do, however, it's just not right for me. For the uninitiated...

It's early. Most are a 6.30am start. It is also very strict. If you join, it is not enough to pay their huge fees and monthly meeting costs, you also have to commit a great deal of time. You are expected to be there every week unless you have a severed limb or worse. If you can't make it, they expect you to find a substitute, a sub. You need to give people referrals. This means that you need to actively find work for others in the room which is very often going to look like irritating the shit out of your friends and relations by having BNI people call them. It means that in order to get your referrals up you'll probably end up getting your house redone, buying people Aloe Vera shit for Christmas and never using who you used to for trade jobs around the house ever again.

You must go on their training courses (more money), join their internal gangs and do talks and potentially, be on the leadership team doing all the bloody work. I tell you, somewhere at the top of this tree is a very very rich person. They make you pay AND they make you run it. Genius. It's very American and ritualised –there are a lot of bollocksy names (think The Apprentice) like Power Team and Titans. People who do good stuff are clapped and given ribbons (I shit you not) and people who do not and flout the rules (read out every week!) are ousted.

All this sounds revolting. And it is. But there is a reason why they are still going, it works. It may be the equivalent of the dodgy handshake brigade but it does bring people business. Many (perfectly normal and lovely!) business people I know have built their entire business via BNI. Referrals of millions are passed around the groups... Doesn't look so bollocksy then does it?

So, if you are invited to one of these shindigs, what to expect? Firstly, expect to be invited! Along with referrals, increasing the size of the group is the mission at BNI. Visitors are gold. There are visitor greeters, visitor coordinators and visitor drives. Sometimes you have to pay a nominal fee for your meal, sometimes not. Have cash in case. Also, take a stack of business cards and a 60 second presentation. You will be wooed, cajoled and persuaded to join. How well /forcefully depends on the group but they want you to join so they will be nice.

There will be some mingling. Now is the moment to grab people or ask for an intro to anyone you really want to speak to. Then it will be a formal, seated meeting with a very fixed structure of talks, educational bits and 60 seconds where each person in turn talks about their business. After this and food, visitors are hustled out the back so the merits of membership can be explained. I've never found this to be an especially hard sell. They know they have to do it so they do their bit but they also know it's not right for everyone and having a non-committed person join isn't going to help them long-term. After this, you will re-join the group as they wrap up and do a touch more mingling. Get any untouched business cards back now! I can't tell you how often I have lost boxes of cards by leaving them as they have gone around a table. Make your escape from this point forth.

Lead with your Ovaries - women's groups, mum's groups
I have only been to a few of these. I am still not entirely comfortable with the whole segregation thing. Don't get me wrong, power to the people, all girls together and all that shizzle, but I am just not sure I see the point of limiting networking to one group of people. And if anyone dare launch "Men's Unlimited, networking for only men" there would be war. Are we women REALLY so delicate we can't talk to men in a room? Really? I like talking to men! I like talking to anyone. I just feel this whole women only thing makes us look weak, like we need something special. Same for mums, black women, lesbian vegans of London (an actual real group at time of writing – my friend accidentally joined when she was trying to join a French Bulldog Group – don't ask me how!) and people over 60. We are all humans. And we are all business people. Why do we need to limit anything? And don't even get me started on the word "Mumpreneur" the vomit is rising even as I type it.

But they then seem to let anyone in anyway. I called up Mums Unlimited "er, I don't actually have kids, can I still come?"

"Oh yes. That's fine. We have men too"

Still mystified. Although not as mystified as the poor woman I talked to on the day when I wasn't quite on my game...

"How old are yours?"

"Oh, two and four"

"Oh, my GOODNESS and you're running a business. That's amazing"

"Well, you know they are quite easy as long as I can take them to the park or the woods for a good run. They just sleep all day"

"All day? Wow. Really? ALL day?"

"Yeah, they just go in their cages and kip. They're no trouble really unless they decide to forage in the bins."

At this point I could see her face had gone kind of ashen and I realised we had been rather talking at cross purposes. I was sure she had said "dog". Clearly, she was thinking children. Children that I was keeping in cages and feeding scraps from the bin. I did hurriedly explain this was not the case and I was describing my Border Collies. Not a moment too soon, she was clearly heading for the loos to call Social Services.

So yes, women's groups. I know several VAs who not only thrive at them but even run their own but I have yet to find one that feels like home for me. But I will keep trying. So far, I have found them to be not businessy enough for my liking – lots of masseuses, acupuncturists, Juice Plus and Aloe Vera sales people. Plus, the odd psychic, an image therapist and a photographer (a requirement of every group) and likely, an accountant and a book-keeper. It's a like a rule! Every group must have an accountant and a photographer, or maybe even several. I'd no idea there was so much work around in the photography arena but either there are lots of very poor photographers out there or there's plenty to go around. Who knew.

Sixty / thirty seconds

When you rock up to a more formal networking gig, they will ask you for your "sixty seconds". This is your opportunity to sell yourself. I'm guessing there are probably whole books on this. I would say, write it, practice it, time it. It sounds simple but it's not a long period of time. The other thing, as well as what you do, is who you do it for. Not "anyone who is a bit busy"! Be specific, as specific as you can. In some BNIs they will ask you to name names of who you want introductions to. Practise it so many times you can do it in your sleep and then when you're asked to do it, you won't be unprepared. I did have in my phone case for about a year a tiny bit of paper with my sixty seconds on it so I would always have it with me in case my mind went blank.

The Rules of Networking

There are whole books on this, none of which I have read (kidding, I have read at least half of one!) on how to network properly. This is my version which basically covers how to make yourself go in the first place and best attempts not to make a total tit of yourself whilst there. If you want to learn how to do it properly to get business, well you'll need to look elsewhere. This is the "check your teeth for spinach and don't get pissed" level of instruction. Make of it what you will.

Rule 1 - it isn't who is in the room it is who they know.
This is actually a real phrase from proper people who know stuff! As previously mentioned, I often have been known to mutter this to myself repeatedly whilst rocking backwards and forwards as I have found myself in the most inappropriate groups of people ever. One day I wondered if I had joined a cult by accident, such was the bizarre mix of people in the room and the activities we took part in. This is what happens.

You turn up. You chat to people and are natural and they say what they do, you tell them what you do. At some point in the future they bump into someone who says "Oh God my PA has pissed off on holiday and totally left me in the shit with this pile of stuff she was meant to do and has forgotten about. My boss wants it by Monday. I'm going to commit Hari Kari with a stapler unless a miracle can be performed." And a helpful person they know (adding to their own kudos at this point FYI) says "D'you know, I met one of those there VA types a while back. She seemed OK. Shall I dig out her card? I bet that's what she does"

This is actually not fiction. To this day, I still have no idea who the bloke was who referred me to this near suicidal, PA-less man and I have done my best to track him down and offer thanks (the job wasn't anything to party about but that isn't the point!).

So, it can work. It does work. It just sometimes feels like you would rather be anywhere else than where you are in that moment. So, fake it! As a wise woman (oh, OK, a columnist in Cosmo) once said "If you can fake an orgasm, you can fake being confident at work". Or in this case you can pretend to give a fuck whilst in a room of people who look like they couldn't SPELL VA let alone hire one. Suck it up buttercup, smile and repeat after me "It's not who's in the room, it's who they know".

Rule 2 – handbags and glad rags

What to wear? It is never an easy call this one. You need to feel comfortable but mostly arriving in PJs is considered a bit off. It depends where you are going. I found one London group was much dressier than another and tweaked accordingly. The key thing is to have somewhere for your business cards if it's a stand and mingle event. The misery of trying to juggle wine, canapés, cards and a conversation is intense. You need a pocket. I now have a networking dress style with pockets. This is not say that whipping a card out from my bra to give someone wasn't a conversation starter, just that it started to get a bit spiky in there once I collected a few (right tit mine, left tit theirs, never let it be said I don't have a system in place!)!

On the topic of boobs, a wise woman told me that us girls should always wear name badges on our right shoulder. Apparently, this will make it easier for men to shake our hands and read our names without getting an eyeful of cleavage. My badges tend only to last five seconds and then be buried under hair but please do try it and let me know if it works. And whether it works for all cup sizes. My rack wouldn't cause a pause for even a sex starved long-term inmate so I am not much help experimentally in this area.

If you can't wear something with pockets and you (quite correctly) think the card in bra thing is a bad idea, next look at your bag. Are you one of these amazing women who can get by with a bag that is smaller than a small car? You are? Wow. Smaller than an A4 pad of paper and not filled with bricks? Good. Chose a bag with a pocket on the outside. Simples. If you have to lug your worldly goods with you then try a bag within a bag so you can abandon most weight at the edge of the room and just keep on you a teeny bag with cards in. Ideally not a clutch bag or again you have the whole juggling thing and it's hard enough talking to strangers without realising you don't have a spare hand to shake or spit an olive pip into.

The other foolish thing I've worn to an event like this is heels. I will give you the thought process:

It's not that far from the tube, I can't be bothered to lug a big enough bag to carry my heels. They aren't that high. I'll just wing it.

The number of idiotic things in those phrases that came back to haunt me as I entered the networking sanctum and met a smiling nervous looking chap ….

"Hello. My name is Gerald and I run an IT business. What is it you do?"
"Me. I bleed for a living. Look at my feet. Is this building really near Bank Tube? Is it? In whose mind, Gerald? And in that mind, was there any thought of signage? No. No there wasn't Gerald. But that's ok because I only want to bleed. I want to walk six thousand fucking miles in shoes that clearly ARE too high for such a distance and BLEED. And then I want to limp to the toilets three floors up and wash my bleeding stumps before limping back down to a room with no bastard chairs where I am expected to stand on my stumps for the next three hours and be fucking nice to people I will never meet again whilst eking out one pitifully small inclusive cocktail with a microbe of gin in it or forking out £12 for a miniscule glass of something actually drinkable. I bet you're glad you're in IT aren't you Gerald? I bet you're glad you're a man and never have to wear shoes that make you want to hack your own toes off with a canapé fork. Am I right Gerald. Am I?"

This is basically all you need to know about footwear and networking. Or going anywhere ever. It might just be me, I know shoes and I have issues but if in doubt, know that really you'd better be in slippers or you will end up in agony. Agony is not good for being a smooth, warm friendly person. Which it what I believe I'm generally aiming for. Not bleeding, screechy harridan. It's a personal thing.

Rule 3 - be a swot

I'm talking Homework people! Pre-and post.

1. Do you know who is going?
2. Do you know what the format is?
3. Can you find the venue (including, if something goes wrong with your phone!)?
4. Do you have a plan?

I must confess at this point that my answer to these is normally;

1. No
2. I'll have a vague idea if I bothered to read the email or have been before
3. Doubtful
4. Hell no

This is not ideal.

It usually involves me arriving late having been lost or failed to find a parking space or both, not having the faintest idea what to expect and most likely missing out on meeting the people I should most be interested in talking to and being trapped in a corner with web developer and a nice lady who sells homemade mosaics. Only yesterday I managed this in quite spectacular style. I blame the localness. If I am going a long way away I actually look at a map and leave lots of time. In my head I can't possibly get lost in the next town (I can and this is proven almost weekly at the moment) and as these towns are in fact in the middle of nowhere, parking is never an issue. Ha!

I stumbled upon a monthly networking group literally ten minutes away that I'd never heard of. At that point, I'd missed it by a day. I put the next date in my diary and a note two weeks prior to that with the weblink to book it. So far, so efficient, right? It gets better. I book. I then request an invoice and pay it that same day. I even manage to order a bloody Secret Santa gift ("under £5, no booze, no food, no giveaways of your own services") to take along. I am so smug I'm glowing at this point. The night before I wrap the gift. I bung it by the front door with my business cards. Magic. I am SUCH a Swotty McSwot PA at heart.

And then cometh the hour, my sat nav lets me down. My timing lets me down (to be fair, it was seven minutes away and I allowed twelve). I get hopelessly lost and the bastarding sat nav is determined to send me to the arse end of nowhere somewhere in what seems to be a whole estate of retirement homes. Once I find the hall (blind luck, I honestly nearly said "fuck it" and went to Costa) I realise I need to pay to park and I have (as usual) got no coins on me so end up doing the pay- by-phone trauma. Pay-by-phone parking to me is as hideous as the self-scan checkouts. I am incapable of getting through it without hitting the wrong button at some point and having to start again. Either I have changed my credit card, or it's expired, or I don't have it on me and can't remember the CVC number, or only my old car is on this particular brand of evil parking hell. Why do there have to be so many different companies? Alternatively, my numeric dyslexia may kick in when I attempt the location number. And, my personal favourite, you know you need the slot that's one to two hours and they ask you for it in minutes. Even I can muster sixty to ninety minutes but I work onsite sometimes and have to park for six, five or seven hours, under pressure whilst talking on my calculator (phone!) multiplying something by sixty unleashes a lot of panic-stricken moments, some sweat and on one notable occasion stomping, swearing and cursing at the robot parking bitch (after entering a new credit card, new reg number AND the location number on about call three by this stage) as I entered too many noughts and parked myself until a week on Thursday for the princely sum of £64, I was not amused.

Anyway, I digress. Don't even start me on packs of aspirin and self-checkouts.

So, I arrive late, I have to park the car with Robot Bitch phone pay, I stumble in. Not in the calm, serene way one should and, basically head for coffee. Lots of coffee. It is 7.30am and I've been up since 5.45am and feel like I have done a day's work already. I more or less snarl at the idiot people who already have coffee but are blocking my way to it. I can feel the growl coming even as I muster a sweet "excuse me, can I just..." in my head "MOVE DICKWAD, MOVE, you have your coffee, get the fuck out of my way you selfish, ignorant twat"

I then neck three coffees on the bounce before attempting to be nice to anyone. I was given a list of who was there and despite that managed to hangout with a lady from the Pru (it transpired we're both on Slimming

World and were considering the "Syns" in a very tiny mince pie "it's fruit!"), a dog behaviourist (on this I am a woman in need, to be fair), a beauty therapist with fabulous hair (kind of pink and silver lines, amazing) and a caterer. And they were lovely, fascinating and enjoyable company but I totally failed to "work the room" and just had a nice chat with some nice people.

So, this is the point where you get some training on how to actually do proper grown up networking. Because clearly, I have no clue. I am though, shit hot at pulling the fat discreetly out of a bacon bap without getting brown sauce up my arms whilst maintaining an intelligent conversation - some things can be taught, others one is born to. If I could teach you I would, but I fear it is a gift.

In the past, I have been better at my planning and at more formal events you often get (or can ask for) the attendee list in advance. Once, I even did the thing you are meant to do and looked through this list and asked the organiser to introduce me to these people. And she did! This is properly how to do it swot style.

At home afterwards I am usually better. At least initially. When I come out having chatted to some folk I will enter their details on my CRM. I will find them on LinkedIn and Twitter. If they need more of a follow up I usually do it. What I then don't do is follow up the follow up. And you need to. Which is a bugger really but you do and I must get better at it. What I can tell you quite clearly not to do are the following things.

Definite networking nos.
1.   Do not add the details of every person who attended an event to your mailing list! Do not! If you had a conversation with them you can ask them the question. Once or twice I have missed people (like one or two in my direct would-be-client sweet spot) that I wanted to speak to and I have sent them a personal message if their email was provided, and said I was so sorry not to have had the chance to chat because blah, that's fine. A spam "it was great to meet you on Thursday" quite clearly sent to two-hundred people is shabby. And obvious. And not cool. Especially when they didn't actually go. Just makes you look like a twonk.

2.   Do not put your newly acquired pile of business cards in a drawer

and ignore them. Also, leaving them in the bottom of your handbag, in the car…. You get what I mean. You need to do something with them, even if it is only to write on it the date of the event and a little note so you remember the conversation "Bad breath guy. Financial planner. Talked about ELO." "New beauty salon owner. Fab hair." "Photographer. Hates weddings, schools, pets, concerts, fetes and events. Only corporates of twenty people or more. Likely go bust in 3 months"

3.   Don't be all mouth no trousers. Keep your promises. If you told someone you know someone you can introduce them to or you recommended a product or an article…. Make sure you do it! And the sooner the better. And write down somewhere (on your CRM system if you use one) what you did and why. That goes for everything. When you meet ten people you know who's who, after a hundred you have no idea. And these people might ring you up! And you are going to have to find some pretty fine bullshit to get through that call if you can't remember who the hell they are. Not that I have ever done that ever of course. Ahem.

Rule 4 – be yourself
If you go into business for yourself then you really need to be yourself. And that goes for who you work with too. Clearly there's lots of versions of you – I wouldn't especially fancy my clients seeing the "11pm on a Friday night in the pub" version of me. It's not appropriate really. But neither do I adopt a 1950's BBC presenter voice and turn into Miss Moneypenny when I turn on the computer. I am still me. I may tone the real me down a smigde when I first meet a client and when I talk to clients I certainly don't swear like the fishwife you by now know me to be, but I should enjoy work and that means having a sense of humour about it. And the best way for me to get clients that work with my personality is to show my actual personality before they sign up! There is really no point in being a different person winning work than you are doing it.

So, when networking, I am myself. I attempt to be the best version of it (clearly doesn't always work with shoes, sat navs, PMT, caffeine lack and robot parking bitches but I try to ignore the screaming evil part of my brain as best I can and slap a smile on).

Rule 5 – don't sell
Again, there are proper books on this malarkey but networking is a long game. I went to one big London meeting and was very entertained to find that several groups of people were actively hiding from a woman who was selling LinkedIn training. It seems she was part of a franchise and they had a very formulaic way of pitching, which she was doing to every person in the place one after the other, she couldn't have been less popular if she'd had herpes. Until you have seen three grown men hide behind a pot plant you haven't lived, FYI. It should be a conversation. Ideally about work but whatever crops up, I've had some wonderfully random conversations with people and they stick in your mind much more than reciting off the same old "what do you do" spiel. And you need to listen as well as talk. It's information passing not selling. And if you can think "what could I do to help this person?" that's a good place to be. And I don't mean sort out their expense receipts! I am thinking of people that might be a good introduction or an article they might find interesting. Being helpful is what PA and VAs are usually very good at and it is a great skill for networking. But again, don't take my word for it, I am usually far too busy scoffing (fatless) bacon butties and trying to scam free cocktails. Read a proper book for God's sake.

Turning them into clients
Lots of this is luck and getting an introduction at the right moment. You've got your fish on a hook, or nearly on a hook. So, what now? Some VAs have highly structed sales processes and systems and documents and so on. I'm quite a lazy bint and have none of these. But a normal sales flow for me goes something like this.

1.   I am introduced to someone with a need or they contact me. If I've been introduced, I'll keep my first contact short and to the point and very light touch. This is easy because I have my value of "whatever is right for the client". This means that I'll talk to anyone, but if I'm not right for them I will suggest or help them find someone that is. I'm pretty open about this and I genuinely mean it. As an added benefit, hopefully it makes me seem less salesy and more helpful.

2.   We have an initial call or meeting. Usually, even if it is a call it is pre-booked. Ahead of this call I will do some research on their company and make some notes in case I go blank. I will tell them prices as early as it seems decent to, mainly so if they can't afford me they don't waste

another twenty minutes of my time. Although again, happy to have that conversation and make sensible suggestions within their budget if I am able to.

3.	I'll follow up. Depending on whether it was a 'maybe' or a 'yes' this will either be straight into a contract and booking a kick off date or confirming prices and a next discussion date. If I am planning to use an Associate on the job I will have mentioned them already and usually would book a second call for them to speak to the client.

4.	If it's to be an ongoing client, we then kick off with a separate onboarding session, or if it's a bit of Ad Hoc work I'll just crack on with it.

That's all totally lovely in an ideal world. You'll be shocked to know that this isn't always how it goes! Sometimes people pick other VAs, they decide they can't afford one or they just vanish into thin air (this happens a lot more than you might count on!)

If they don't sign up there and then, it is good to keep in touch with them on a regular basis. The bugger of being a VA is that the people who need us are overwhelmed by work. That's why they need us. This is also why it takes them a month to return a phone call. Often these are slow burners and you just have to be patient. There is a very tricky line between following up and stalking so you need to be smart about it.

Associates

For a lot of VAs, myself included, working as an associate to another VA is a great way to test the waters. Essentially, you are subcontracted to another VA who has too much work on. This can either be on a task by task basis, literally "Can someone help me format a Word document by the end of today" or as an ongoing role with one specific client. I've done both and I have associates working with me in both ways now that I am too busy to do it all myself.

The Ad Hoc stuff is brilliant. This is how you can transition into being a VA whilst still holding down a fulltime job because you only accept the work when you have time to do it. If you are able to get to know some well-established VAs when they are all of a sudden up to their eyes, you can step in, do a task of an evening, send it back. Bob's your uncle, submit invoice as agreed. As long as the other VA knows what you are able to do, they can send you work that can be done around your other job. This is much easier to manage through another VA than directly with a client. They know what the score is and have quite possibly been in a similar situation.

And it somehow feels a bit weird talking to direct clients about your "proper job" – as if they are getting the dregs while you are trying to juggle. Taking on associate work is a great way to get some practise and some income and along the way you can soak up some knowledge about how different VAs work and the type of clients they have. It's also great if you have specialist skills. For example, I work with one VA who is my go-to social media girl and I have a chap who is my go-to Excel guy. I also know VAs who can build a website from scratch and others who actually like Infusionsoft rather than thinking it is an invention of the Devil. If you have a strong skillset, a specialism (languages) or just love doing something – like transcription or writing then you can become known as an expert in that realm and that can result in lots of referrals and more interesting work coming your way. More on this in Niches.

If you choose to have a longer-term role as an associate then this can be great, or not so great! In this case, you will normally work much closer with the end client, the main VA having either handed this over to you or drafted you in specially for this role. The lead VA will have less of a day to day impact and you'll do most communication with the end client, based on guidance from the lead VA of course.

The plus sides of any associate work are many. You don't have any cost of sale. The work appears, you do it and you haven't had to go and win it yourself. I know some VAs who only work this way because they don't fancy the networking and negotiating and general trauma that direct clients can bring or, they aren't in the market for a fulltime VA job because they already do something else so they just pick up bits here and there.

You also work in a team and have someone to talk to. Do not knock this! It can be really lonely when it is just you and a client. When the client isn't yours you get to have a step back and don't have all the responsibility yourself, if you are stuck or they are being awkward or whatever then you have someone to call. Even if it's only just a rant to get it off your chest and then you grit your teeth and do whatever it was you were bitching about anyway! Most other VAs are very generous with their time and experience so building up a close relationship with them is a no-brainer anyway for any insanely stupid questions you may need to pick their brains about any other VA work.

The obvious downside of associate work is that you earn less. The lead VA found the work, they are managing the client relationship and they take a margin so your rate will be less. For this reason, some new VAs decide never to do any associate work. I still do some associate work now as do several other VAs I know who have been at this way longer than I have. The money isn't at my full rate for those jobs but they bring me other things that I don't get elsewhere so it balances when I look at my work life as a whole. I review it fairly regularly and agonise at least twice a week in the middle of my usual hours agonising about whether I am making the right choices.

Now there is earning less and earning a pittance! Once your rate is set, you might also set an associate rate, or a rate that you will not go below, but bear in mind that a guaranteed number of hours a month is a good thing, and worth losing a couple of quid for. Be warned though that there are some agencies out there that pay very low rates to their associates. It doesn't matter who you are working for, you are now self-employed and have costs! Your hourly rate should bear no resemblance to anything like a temp hourly rate, that's not how this works. Of course, when you start you take anything, but just be a bit cautious if you're taking on large amounts of hours at a very low rate because you'll never have time to go out and sell to new clients who can pay your, higher, direct rate.

And how should you behave as an associate? Well, basically you treat the VA as what they are, a client. You communicate in a timely way, do what you are asked to in terms of invoicing and paperwork and you always remember that this is their valuable client. They did the marketing, the endless bastard networking meetings and all the leg work for this to come off. It doesn't matter how totally amazing that end client thinks you are for doing the work you do not ever think you can entice them away. Firstly, there will most likely be a legal agreement in place forbidding you from doing this. Second, it's hideously wrong and you aren't in business to screw people over, are you? I've heard that this has happened to other VAs. Happily I've never seen it myself. All the VAs I've ever had any involvement with have had good moral codes and it wouldn't even cross their minds. I'm just putting it out there really obviously in case it isn't clear "thou shalt not steal another VAs client". And obviously, you do the same excellent work that you would at any other time.

There are a few grey areas when working as an associate – if you want a reference it should really be the VA that gives it but it's likely more to be meaningful and useful if it comes from the end client (after all, they are the ones seeing your work). But then you can't say that they are your client and bung a nice testimonial up on your website to that effect, because they aren't. So, best thing is to be open and ask the VA.

You should expect to sign a contract when you start working with another VA and in some cases, they may ask you to agree to specific ways of working as well. I have this for associates I work with, it is a way of me making the experience for my clients as uniform as possible. For example, they might ask that you only use their email address for corresponding with the client rather than using your own business email which can confuse clients. Not that clients are daft. They understand (ish!) that VAs subcontract out as they don't have the capacity to do everything themselves but it shows a much more professional finish. Lots is common sense. If you are using your phone for work and give out the number to clients or contacts, then don't have a "cute" voicemail recorded by your five-year-old saying "mummy is busy". Not business appropriate. Neither is selling your Aloe Vera or Juice Plus shit to my clients. Just FYI.

MEETINGS

I've always been a punctual person. Some might say too punctual. I used to arrive for things ages early and had to lurk somewhere until a reasonable time before announcing myself. Since self-employment, this happy trait has left me. I don't exactly know how or why, I suspect it is because my days are insanely busy and I now count every unbilled minute as a personal failure. Ten minutes sitting in a car park is a no no.

Plus, clients seem to develop an unhelpful psychic power and ring me just as I am about to get ready to go out of the door. That's my excuse. I now have to remind myself that I need to arrive fifteen minutes early for whatever is it. This is because no one counts your arrival from the time you rock up in the car park or at the nearest tube – I need to allow time to get from the vehicle to the building! Once in the building I will almost certainly need to find a loo as I have the bladder capacity of a gnat. Even if the drive only took me twenty minutes and I went before I left the house, I will need to go again. Plus, it might be wise to do a quick check in the mirror for lipstick on or spinach in teeth and give the hair a quick brush. Of course, this doesn't work so well if you are going to a client's house. I was most proud of myself for arriving ten minutes early but then, for the sake of courtesy, didn't want to knock on the door early so sat in my car, on their drive, looking like a fish in a bowl until they came out to check I wasn't somehow paralysed or fallen foul to a central locking crisis.

Client onboarding sessions

The internet is a wonderful thing. But it also does have the ability to scare a person shitless.

Take the many VA Forums on Facebook. Some of the questions on there would fry your noodle. Not merely because you don't know the answer, but because it has never even occurred to ask the question in the first place. My favourite of these, which after two years I finally got my arse together on, recently is Client Onboarding.

The very phrase sent terror through my veins. I mean, what is it? I have clients, if they aren't onboard, are they off board? I mean, am I missing something here that every other bugger knows about and I don't?
Cue a long, perplexing and remarkably frustrating Google search that got me no closer to an answer on what the hell this onboarding jobbie is and why I should do it.

In the end, as with much of my VA life, I realised I sort of have been doing it but very much in a non-structured way (for which read "making it up as I went along"). My initial client kick off session would be poshly called an Onboarding Session if you want to be fancy pants. Was it the same for everyone? No. Was it perfect? Not always. Did anyone suffer for the lack of an official onboarding process? Most likely not.

But, having tail-spinned myself into a blind panic, I created myself a Word document sparkily named "Client Onboarding Document" and added to it everything I might possible need to know about a new client, how they work, any software and passwords, any regular tasks I need to schedule – basically a download of as much of their brain as I can get. I also have a money laundering check in there if I'm doing anything vaguely book-keepery. This is a current joy of many a VA. HMRC have declared in their wisdom that VAs that do book-keeping need to register for the Anti-Money Laundering Wotsit. For this we have to pay a stupid amount of money and then do the required checks on our clients which makes us look like suspicious arseholes. There are many huge traumas with this registry. Firstly, no one at HMRC can actually define what tasks fall under "book-keepery" and therefore who and what definitively falls under this law.

Occasionally an urban myth spews out a tale that as long as you only type up the invoice and don't do the maths you don't need to register. I mean, what the actual fuck? Does typing expense receipts into a spreadsheet count? Marking an invoice as paid? The truth is that at time of writing no one really has the faintest idea. Not least the muppets actually making the rules. So, I have registered on the basis that I'd rather be safe than sorry, especially as I access Xero accounting system for several clients. But that isn't to say it doesn't piss me off a lot whenever I think about it too hard. That money would buy me a lot of holiday cocktails.

So now, when I have a kick off meeting with a new client I have a list to work through. And I call it, ta dah, my Onboarding Process. This makes me feel like a proper grown up VA. Right up until I read the next post on Facebook that says, "How do you blah blah blah" and I realise that I don't do whatever blah blah is and never have. Sigh.

Reviews with clients

I typically talk to my clients weekly or fortnightly so I don't tend to book official reviews as such. I hope that we normally will communicate. I do fix review meetings for clients who are looked after by associates. Usually six monthly after an initial review.

I generally approach these meetings with total dread and horror. I still don't quite know why. I think it all falls into the camp of having to be a grown up. I know lots of VAs that regularly conduct client reviews without it becoming an emotionally draining trauma but I'm just not there yet. It's like an appraisal, only worse.

All it is (again, I could send myself nuts wondering what others do and if I am doing it right) is "how's it going for you?" and if I or the associate have any feedback or requests we'll look at those.

This is a good opportunity to amend a retainer contract if the hours needed have changed. Or, for Ad Hoc clients it might be more cost effective for them to move to retainer. I typically put all new clients on Ad Hoc while we work out what needs doing. After three months, we can review and either move them onto retainer or leave them as it. It's OK when you have someone that has worked with a VA before or has a very clear idea of tasks but it is easy for clients to wildly overestimate how much they have got to handover. It feels like a mountain of work to them but often, that's a perception because they are overwhelmed rather than a cold calculated amount of time required.

My other challenge to myself at the three-month mark is to ask for some feedback in the form of a testimonial. I use them on my website and also, it reassures my needy soul that they really do value what I am doing! If possible, I'll also get them to do a LinkedIn review as well.

Sales meetings

I never really think of meetings as sales meetings. This is in part because it would be yet another reason to have a meltdown! But really, I am just getting to know someone and their business and they are getting to know me and mine. I have had first meetings where I knew that there was an opportunity for work and tried to be very prescriptive and work through a process, but it felt horrible.

I do some research on the person I am speaking to, write down some hopefully intelligent questions to ask if my mind goes blank and just play it by ear. To date, I have only had one meeting (by phone as it goes) where I really struggled and felt I was rubbish. I did a bit of analysis afterwards (with wine) and worked out that this was largely because the chap I was talking to had the personality of wet cardboard (as verified by another VA who also "met" him about the same work). Could I have done better? Yes. Am I going to weep and wail over it? No, because I don't want a client that I have to talk to once a week where the conversation is going to be like getting blood out of a stone. Life is too short. One thing to bear in mind though, this is a meeting. A discovery meeting. A getting to know you meeting. A chemistry meeting. Call it what you will. It is not an interview, (see the section on Employee Versus Business Owner).

Meetings with myself

Yep, I have internal meetings. Clearly, it's a right bitch trying to coordinate diaries and make it work for everyone! Seriously, I do have meetings with myself. Quarterly and annually I hold an official company meeting, I don't change location and I don't even get a posher coffee but I do work through an agenda. Tragic but true. After a while, I realised that I am so busy doing work, that I had no clue how I was doing, either as a business or even for myself. I was too busy doing it to feel it. I decided that summing up the business as "solvent - I think" and my view of life as "pretty knackered actually" wasn't really enough in the way of data. So, I take a half day quarterly, a day every year, and I look at a list of things I want to review, assess them, do some pretty graphs on the numbers (shudder), think about new, existing and ex clients and what if anything I can learn from them and my experience of working with them.

My minutes are a scream. I do believe last year the word "cockwomble" featured several times, along with "shitty stick" and "flaky-bloody-life-coaches". I look at my marketing, the networking and events I go to and review if they are getting me anywhere. I assess how many hours I've worked (obviously, no event is complete without an obsess over the billables!) and how I am feeling about the business. If I have made mistakes (it happens), I try to work out how and why and resolve to just move on if nothing can be done. Again, the minutes have read "what the fuck was I THINKING?" – to the point I felt, no point fluffing it up when I'm the only one reading it and I know I ballsed up. I'll review my associates and decide if I need to be looking for any more in the coming months.

Basically, I look at everything. Well, except the stationery bill, there are some things that a girl should remain in denial about for eternity. I like pens OK? And bullet journals. And coloured shiny things. I decide what I can improve on and what my goals should be for the next quarter or year. Now that makes me sound terrifyingly grown up. I didn't do this for a long time and felt vaguely like I was driving a car in sunglasses in the dark. I am much happier now I have a clear path and I know what I am meant to be doing. Do I hit all my targets? No. But I'll be more or less doing the tasks that I think will get me there at some point.

Don't misunderstand me, holding a meeting with yourself is a bloody difficult thing. I do end up talking to myself a lot, out loud, or to a nearby animal. I feel like a total knobend as I read my agenda items to myself and the closest collie (who ignores me, not having heard the word "biscuit" at any point) but it is important. Have a look at the Support section for ways not to talk to yourself like a crazy person.

BIG GIRL PANTS – THE CHALLENGING TIMES OF BEING YOUR OWN BOSS

For all the delights that being self-employed brings, there are some occasions when I just long for the days of having a proper job. Because it isn't all coffee and working in your PJs. As I've said before, but it bears repeating because it genuinely didn't sink into my subconscious for a stupid amount of time, 'if I no work, I no make money'. No work, no money.

Holidays

We all love a holiday and we all remember the stress of having to get everything finished before the holiday so you could go away with just a little hope that you wouldn't either return to carnage or get called while you were away. That stress pales into insignificance when you are self-employed let me tell you. One colleague (self-employed but not a VA), tells me she hasn't even HAD a holiday since working for herself because the horror not being paid for a week is too much to bear.

So, you have to save up your pennies to pay for your holidays, same as normal. But you aren't earning any either while you are away, so your month's takings are going to be down by a week or two weeks depending on how long you take. The alternative is, if all your work is retained, so you do a fixed twenty hours for client A, ten for client B, twenty for client C then you might be OK BUT you have to fit those hours into whatever time is left in the month. So basically fit four weeks' work into three or even two. Good luck with that! Or you get into "can we roll the hours to next month?" which all starts getting messy and annoying as you then have to do extra hours the next month - another reason I'm not a fan of the retainer.

And remember that this is now your business! Can you afford not to check your emails while you are away? What if a new prospect got in touch? Would you want them to just get an out of office response and then leave them for a week? Some VAs take on another VA to cover for them when they are on holiday to deal with their inbox. That's a massive level of trust, lovely as we all are, that's a lot of information about your business you are effectively giving a 'competitor'. Plus, having that cover costs money. If they help you with your client work, that's billable back so you are at least making a cut of that. But anything they do on your business is entirely a cost to you. So, you aren't earning and you are paying someone else. So currently I'd rather save that money for Pina Coladas at the beach and check my emails a few times a day in case of a crisis. I find I can combine email checking AND Pina Coladas. I'm nothing if not efficient!

Once I did have to take a client call and deal with an associate issue on holiday. All of which I would really rather not have done, but what can you do? That kind of thing isn't easily to delegate. And he's a lovely chap and it was a misunderstanding and a bit of a balls up. It took three hours out of my holiday, caused a modicum of swearing but if I had left that until my return he might have gone from mildly peeved to totally livid. It just isn't worth it for the sake of being militant about holiday time.

Illness

As I write this section, I am currently lying flat on my back with a herniated disc. This started on holiday in actual fact but was entirely unrelated to Pina Colada consumption (or mojitos, or beer or other beverages at all). When I limped back from holiday, sobbing with the pain and unable to even think, let alone consider work, the only thought in my head was "Oh God how I wish I had a job I could phone in sick to".

Of course, I can phone in sick to all my clients, it'd take a bit of unravelling, none of which I had the braincells for on the cocktail of drugs I was on. But again, if I am not working, I am not being paid. And this helpfully happened after a holiday so I'd already lost ten days or so of earnings.

So, here I am, largely bed bound, doing client work in chunks around pain management and drugs that make me high as a kite and/or make me pass out. It is not ideal. But suck it up I must. If I had my old job I would have called in sick totally guilt-free for the foreseeable (maybe nobly doing a bit here and there just so as not to come back to carnage), got sent some nice flowers and laid myself out to binge watch Breaking Bad for a fortnight until I got some treatment. Oh God, how lovely that sounds.

As it is, I have moved myself back to my parents so they can look after the dogs and all aspects of life that I can't (cooking, washing) so that in the moments when I am able to function, I can just focus on work. And I am working the best I can. My clients are adorable and being sympathetic to the best of their abilities but they still have deadlines. Which means I have to grit my teeth and get on with it, despite the pain, and despite the pain making me rather grouchy (I have had to add a daily task to my list which is to check all my timesheet entries after I discovered one that said "Telling that silly cow at XXX for the third time that, yes, she does have to post it" and another that said "wading through usual piles of crap". These are not the kind of thing you want to inadvertently send a client at the end of the month with an invoice. Drugs or no!)

What if I really couldn't work? What if, despite the drugs I was incapable? What if I fell under a bus – who would even know who my clients were to let them know? I think this is why one should have an emergency plan. I say "one" because I clearly don't have one but should. Really there should be on my desk an envelope "in the event of my death" with all my log in details, who my clients are so an email can be sent

"Dear Client,
sorry but your VA was hit by a bus and will not be working for you anymore. So sorry to give you this news.

Kind regards,

Random friend of your late VA.

PS the executor of the will might send you an invoice if they can understand the timesheet system to create one.

PPS If you'd like to come to the funeral, let us know and we'll give you the details"

I really should have an emergency plan! Right, that's going on the task list. But then it would need to be kept up to date as well. Oh, hell what a faff. See, even when you're dead running your own business is exhausting!

The bright side to this is that when sick, home working is certainly easier to manage than working in an office with a commute. It is much less exhausting. But all the things I do go out for are quite important – new client meetings, networking, working on, going to the post office (which actually gets right on my tits so I'm not the least gutted about that being off the cards for a bit). But it is still hard.

On day two of my back injury I had a Skype meeting with a prospective new client. I really wanted this gig. There was no way I was going to cancel as it had been put in ages before because of my holiday. It's a Skype, I had to get actually dressed and put on make-up. At this stage I hadn't got my pain relief properly sorted out and to say I was in agony doesn't begin to describe it. Even the thought of sitting at my dressing table to slap on some lippy filled me with horror. I didn't feel I could do the Skype from bed and decided to do it standing at my desk which was marginally less awful for my back than sitting.

At the appointed time, we hooked up. Thank GOD, she went video-less because what she would have seen during the course of the next hour was me writhing, actually writhing doubled up in pain. And pacing the house. And grimacing. And after forty-five minutes, tears streaming down my face and crawling round the floor. And yet talking quite normally and more or less intelligently. At the end of the call I did confess that I was suffering and hoped that I hadn't sounded too drugged up. It seems not but she might have been being nice and assumed I was just a total loon. When we finally stopped talking I rolled onto my back and howled in pain. That is the level of dedication needed to run your own business, I think that was "worst thing you have ever had to do to have your own business" moment. And, as an aside, naturally, because I was on a very key call, I had two lots of people come to the fucking door as well. One was my totally adorable and kind neighbour with my drugs from the chemist who let herself in and just started a conversation with me, assuming I was in bed, having not spotted my text about the very very important call I would be on when she came back and the other was a lovely man returning my dogs having taken them for a walk for me.

And do you know what? A week later I had an email. I won that client. Would I have won it if I had postponed? Quite possibly not. It was worth the pain.

I know two other VAs this week also off having various operations. And they will be off for the most miniscule amount of time because they simply can't afford to recuperate any longer. For planned things where you know there is going to be a serious amount of away time then you can put in place associates to carry on the work. At least then you are getting some revenue, but anything run of the mill, the basic concept is 'suck it up'.

Babies

I thankfully haven't had to tackle the thorny issue of maternity leave – there's tax stuff, work stuff, oh man. In an old job, I was PA to a business owner who was pregnant with her first child. She called me from a cab and casually said;

"I don't want anyone to panic but I think I might be in labour. Can you give it an hour and call my husband and tell him to bring my bag to the hospital?"

"Er, should you not be going to the hospital. Like now? Why an hour? You're not seriously considering doing what I think you're doing? Let me call them and rebook, it'll be fine"
"It's a very important meeting and it's only an hour. I'll be fine. It's only

a few contractions. Soon as I'm done I'll hop in a cab to the Portland"
"YOU'RE IN LABOUR! You can't do a sales meeting while you are in labour, you're insane!"

And, yet she did. Cool as a fucking cucumber, went to the meeting, in labour, sold a half million-pound project and then went off to have her baby. And it can't have been much more than an hour after the birth that she was on the phone giving me a list of instructions. When it is your business, you can't just switch off.

I know VAs that have had babies and made it work AND even managed to grow their business whilst on mat leave but I think I'll be keeping my legs firmly crossed, life is quite complicated enough.

However, many VAs have remarkably successful businesses and have small children. Often it's the reason people become VAs – the ability to work flexibly around their children's' needs. Hats off to them, I don't know how they manage. Not having kids, I don't really know how people make it work (apart from childcare being a total necessity!) but there is plenty of support out there if you are worried about how it all fits.

Mistakes

Oh, I hate it when things go wrong. I realise that it is part and parcel of being a human and not a robot, but still. It's that hideous feeling in your tummy. Something has gone horribly wrong and it may very well have been my fault...

I think every PA has had that moment. A call comes in. Someone is somewhere they shouldn't be or a week early or an hour late or the flight left an hour ago without the key person on it. We've all been there. You get the call. You go hot. Cold. Hot again. You sweat a bit and your breathing gets shallow. The world narrows to a pinprick and your future flashes before you. You see yourself sitting on a curb selling the Big Issue with a ratty looking dog on a bit of string. Your stomach starts doing all manner of weird things. Then you begin the email search. The search that will tell you whether this current hideous situation is in fact of your making or not. If not, happy days! You fist pump the air. You call your boss back, try not to sound too gleeful as you explain what happened without actually using the phrase "It wasn't me! It was them, the dickheads!" and nobly work to fix the problem in your usual way.

Sometimes though. It was you. You wonder if you can magic yourself dead by the power of thought alone or quickly elope. But you can't. And as you realise that, hope goes out of the window and you know you have to do it – fess up. This is actually much worse if the disaster has yet to be discovered as you are telling them from scratch. Either way, it's as much fun as chewing cold vomit. You just have to man up, apologise and be as efficient as you possibly can, rectifying the disaster, whatever it may be.

Disasters are no better in the world of VAs. Maybe a client can fire you easier if you've pulled a real humdinger, but the feelings are pretty much the same. What I find is harder to deal with is a complaint from a client about an associate. I am in the middle trying to find the truth of what actually happened and smoothing it over. I used to be a restaurant manager, when people complained then I ran the risk of having garlic bread or beer thrown at my head, by comparison, mere verbal complaints are pretty tame. But what I struggle with is the lack of control. If I had cocked up, it would be down to me and I could then be sure I didn't do it again, I have to trust that my associate will do the same. That's quite hard.

Non-payers

I have so far been relatively lucky in this respect. The large majority of my clients pay me on the day or the day after I send my invoice, I kid you not. I have great clients! But, on occasion, I have had challenges with Ad Hoc clients who haven't paid and it is ludicrously stressful.

No one likes a nag so there is a fine line between chasing for what you are owed and becoming a pain in the arse. Many VAs circumvent this trauma by setting retained clients up with an automatic payment, then at least they are only chasing for extras. Iffy cashflow, especially if you are paying associates, can be a total nightmare.

In a strange way, it (for me anyway) becomes easier once the relationship has totally broken down. Think of it this way, you are working with this client day in, day out but they owe you money. At what point do you stop working until they pay what they owe? It's really very hard. But, for a one-off job or where you are pretty sure there is no intention of paying or ever working with you again, you can bring out the big guns. Sad but true, I've had to threaten two non-payers with court action. Both paid up that same day (small claims court, fill in the forms, screenshot and email – no need to pay unless you submit the form). But would I, could I do that with a client I was still working with? No, probably not, it's just too hard for the relationship.

In one of these cases, the client was having massive cash flow issues and it was more a case of can't than won't. The other was a part non-payment because the client didn't feel she had to pay for offsite work (yep, really – she only wanted to pay for the time work was done onsite and just paid that bit of the invoice. The outstanding amount wasn't very much but I still had to pay the associate for that time. It is the principle of the thing; it's an invoice with supporting timesheet not a suggested donation amount - FFS, you don't just pay whatever you feel like!). This is the kind of bollocks you have to deal with when you are self-employed. It falls very heavily into the Not Much Fun category.

By contrast with others, I'm doing well. I have never had a debt unpaid. But, it sure has made me smarter about getting payment upfront when I start with someone new.

Endings

On the subject of clients that get on your tits...

At some point, there will come a time when you have to let a client go. This might be with sadness because through no fault on either side it just isn't the right work for you anymore, you don't have enough hours or it no longer fits your skillset. Or it might be because they have driven you entirely crazy and the moment of leaving prompts you to skip around the room with glee. I parted ways with one client after a very brief period and I have to confess that abandoning ship was one of the most liberating moments of my life. I still grin from ear to ear when I remember that feeling. Petrified but triumphant!

In the case of the first example, obviously, it is important to make your exit with courtesy and skill (example two - eat my dust sucker! I jest, I was obviously a total professional, they never saw my happy dance or the bottle of fizz I opened seven seconds after the email left my outbox).

The main thing is to ensure that the client ends up with someone who is right for them. If you look after them directly then you can go one of several ways. You might decide to have an associate look after them. Then they are still on your books but you aren't doing the work and you make a margin. This might take a very skilfully worded discussion and some careful management, but it can be done. If they are just not right for your business and you want a fresh start, then you might find them a replacement. You might even ask for a finder's fee from the new VA for the introduction. Or you can offer to ask your network and let the soon-to-be-ex client do the searching themselves. You'll know what feels right in any given circumstance.

It is the nature of freelance work that clients come and go. The flexibility for the client is what makes it such an attractive option so it is inevitable that clients will move on away from you as the needs of their business change. My favourite kind of ending is because they have got too busy for me and are having to move to an employed member of staff, this feels like a success even as it ends. A client may also simply change VA which could mean you need to train your own replacement. I've not had to do this (yet – I daresay it will happen at some point) but all you can do is the best you can to handover absolutely everything and be helpful.

SUPPORT

One of the first things you realise a couple of months into being your own boss is that it's lonely at the top. Even if you are the top, middle and bottom of your own personal business hierarchy. Me, myself and I as the saying goes.

I speak to more people now than I did when I was employed (my last job was also home based, I'm not an antisocial cow) but I don't have someone who I can moan to at the water cooler. There is support out there but, the buck stops with you and it can get very lonely, especially if you are used to a buzzing office and having lots of people around. This can be soul destroying when you first set up and you don't have much client work. Fear not, it does get easier. Once you have client work, your days get so much busier you will have no time to care whether you see another soul in the next forty-eight hours or not.

In those early days, you need to get some structure around your days. Treat your own work as if it was client work. Give yourself a deadline – it doesn't matter if it's irrelevant. Set targets that are achievable and if you really are in the mire of despair, just do three easy simple things in a day so you have some things to tick off. This book would never have been finished if I hadn't given myself a tough deadline because client work always comes first. It is so easy to just waft along on your own stuff because it doesn't land in the Urgent square. Getting used to prioritising your own workload can be tough if you've never done it before but it can be fun. There are many apps and systems and much lovely stationery to help you, should you be stuck!

I am lucky enough to have an amazing support network of family, friends and a local group of business people and still sometimes my work life feels like a wasteland of loneliness in which the opportunities for me to balls up get greater every day. It does get easier. When I started, my poor best friend used to have to check every invoice I sent out because I was so paranoid about my ability to manage it on my own. Happily for both of us, I'm past that now but there are still things that I have doubts and worries about and it just doesn't feel the same as being in a job where you can check stuff out with someone if you're in a quandary. And regardless of who you talk to, no one is ever quite right – your loved ones believe in you but quite possibly have no real clue about the world you work in (even if you do bore them shitless about it most days; trust me, they lost the will to live, let alone listen months ago). You meet other VAs and they are amazing (we'll come to them) but effectively they are competitors and they may very well have different ideas as to how to make things work. And others aren't necessarily the right people to open up to. So, the best bet is really to have a big network that you can call on when you need advice and support or a good old fashioned kick up the arse.

And remember that this works both ways. Being happy to make use of support does mean that you need to give back where needed, I think of it as karma. Being generous (in a managed and not totally stupid way) with advice and help where you can is as good for you as it is for others. I met a new VA at a networking event once and gave her my card and told her to call me if she was ever stuck. Months later she rang. Naturally I had totally forgotten about her but she had a random question about something. She was a smart cookie, she'd asked Google already and come up with a million too many answers so she remembered me and called. Good on her. I solved her dilemma in about 60 seconds flat. She got her answer and was happy, I felt my halo glowing for a few hours. It's all good. And on that subject...

VAs play nice

We really do. One of the real eye openers for me was the collaborative nature of the industry. We are all, technically competitors but we get on, we give each other help, a laugh. It's truly brilliant. I know some VAs in "real life" and some only virtually from Facebook Groups dedicated to VAs. I have made some amazing friends in these groups and on the rare occasions when we get together the screeching, hugging and nattering (and prosecco drinking) is insane.

As a bit of a warning, not all FB groups are created equal. Some are open to anyone which means that whatever you put out in them can be seen widely, even potentially by clients or friends of clients. Bear that in mind before you share your soul, or more likely a dilemma with a git of a client. Some groups have loads of people on them that aren't actually VAs, they just hang out, I don't know why, maybe because we're fun and we know stuff. Seriously, you can ask a very techie questions and someone will know the answer, it's amazing. And people will help! But this means that you don't know who is reading your posts and comments. So mind your manners.

Also, some of these groups are based in the USA. Nothing against the USA at all but they do work quite a differently than the UK and reading their stuff can drive me totally mental. There was one poor girl (I say poor girl, what I really mean is stupid cow – hey, I can't be nice all the time, it's unnatural) in the US, delighted about having just got a job on Fivver which was paying $6 an hour. Yup, that is SIX US dollars an hour. That's less than £5 an hour in UK money! It is below THEIR minimum employed wage (which someone pointed out and got totally shouted at for "ruining the happy vibe" or some such bollocks) never mind below a freelance rate. So, it can wind me up. The more these idiots are prepared to work for slave labour rates, the harder it is for those of us with enough wit to charge sensible amounts to find clients. It devalues everyone. And they do largely seem to be much more about tasks and software than us UK folks. So, read with caution!

Also, most groups have been set up by someone who is selling you something. Not all, but most. Because moderating a group is a total pain and why would someone do it out of the goodness of their heart? They don't, it's a sales funnel. And that is totally fine as long as you are aware of it.

Groups and training

So, we've looked a bit at Facebook groups. There are some "official" VA things you can join. Some are more official than others. I have only limited experience with these and they change all the time so it's worth doing some research to keep current with what there is out there.

As far as I know, at time of writing the biggest (1,600 members) UK group of VAs is the Society of Virtual Assistants set up in 2005 by a group of Scottish VAs. There is a paid or a free membership. They also run an annual survey of the UK industry and the report is well worth getting your paws on if you can. Potential clients can search a list of approved members and there are lots of resources for VAs setting up. I'm not a member. It's vaguely on my list of things to do but I've never got to it. In order to be approved you seem to need to use a landline number for your business. I haven't used a landline in my house since 2007 and I've no intention of starting now, if it wasn't for the broadband I wouldn't have it at all. Given that you can now get a VOIP number and route it to your PC I hardly see how it can be any guarantee to a client of you not being a fly-by-night scoundrel anyway. I'm not good with rules that I see as pointless! But, my business, my choice. I don't need to join. Hurrah! (But I religiously complete the survey because I think it's seriously useful to give and receive some industry data and I will happily pay for that).

One group I have joined because it suits my ethos is VIP VA. Again, great Facebook group. VIP VA was set up to champion high standards in the VA industry in the UK (kind of the anti $6 USA per hour brigade!) and there were some hoops to jump through but none that I had any issues with. It is all about providing quality and that does mean getting your ducks in a line on data protection and contracts etc. The group gives massive amounts of support and also access to a private, members-only group where I feel safe to have very open conversations or just a rant when my day has gone to total shit. It is very liberating having a group of like-minded people to chat to and pick the brains of when you are stuck. I think of this lot as my Tribe and when we get together from all parts of the UK (and France!) it's going to be messy but bloody good fun. Again, clients can contact VIP VA to be matched with a VA and so far, my experience of this has been really smooth. It's the easiest sales process in the world. There is also a training programme now for new VAs and a mentoring system for newbies and old, drained jaded witches like myself!

There are LOADS of VA training programmes available. As I said, I did none. I probably did make life harder for myself by just winging it. So, because I haven't done any, I can't recommend any particular courses but there are oodles more out there. If you are looking for one, I would suggest that ideally you want one where you are getting some direct interaction with the trainer plus a group at the same stage as you that you can buddy with. If you just want to work on your own buy a book. You almost might as well just get free resources and do it yourself.

Coaches, buddies and mentors

I was really lucky to have 2 local VAs to annoy the shit out of when I started. Then there are also online groups to badger for ideas. Having said that, no one appreciates a "I'm just starting up, what do I do?" post. I mean, narrow it down a bit! What I would have liked and would have got if I had done a training course, is a gang at the same place as me. It would have been nice. I know loads of VAs now but it would have been bloody brilliant to have had a newbie at the same point as me to have a moan to and bounce ideas off. This to me is a real plus of training courses - a built-in buddy system. Obviously, you might hate your fellow trainees but probably not all of them!

A buddy system is a great thing. I know several VAs who have one – not necessarily a VA either but someone working in a similar freelance business. Having someone to be accountable to is really important when you work alone. Clearly, you have to deliver client work so that gets done, always, and always first. The challenge is that your own stuff falls further and further down the list the busier you get. A buddy can hold you accountable to your own goals and you can do the same for them. You might have a success milestone or you might just nag each other every week or fortnight. Either way, it is a very good way to make sure you focus on your business. I have just started this, rather bizarrely with a former client. So far, it's brilliant. We each create lists of what we need to achieve and by when. I certainly do feel a bit more likely to do that annoying task if I know she's going to say on a Friday morning "Still? Really? It's only going to take five minutes. What's stopping you?".

The other way to work on yourself and your business is to have a coach. There is a coach for everything and used at the right time in the right way they can be a superb form of development. There are ones for VAs, like Charlotte Wibberley who wrote the foreword to this book or there are a huge variety of other ones. Be warned! When you go out in the world of networking you will meet SO many coaches. So many. And they go from one extreme to the other. Some may be part of a franchise aimed at small businesses which has a very structured (I may have to use the phrase "Americanised Bollocks", I apologise) methodology and some may be more fluffy life coaches who are going to surround you in incense and wave angel cards at your inner child. Whatever floats your boat, but if you decide to work with a coach, it is a big investment in money and time so make very sure they are right for you. Ideally, talk to several people who have finished a course or whatever the programme is and get their feedback. It may be that you need to focus on business goals, or personal presentation skills (like giving a talk) or it may be something else entirely. I work with a lot of coaches (I am their VA, I don't have a posse of my own coaches, although if I win the lottery I totally would! And a gardener, housekeeper, cook and a personal trainer) and they work with high performing people. There's a bit of a myth that only people that don't know what they are doing need coaching. Far from it, the chaps my chaps work with are top of their game and performing at 97% brilliance – the coaching is to give them the extra 3%.

I did a few sessions a couple of years into my VA journey just to check in, assess what was working, what wasn't and where I wanted to be. Remember, in a normal role you'd have an appraisal to do these things – it's a bit of a challenge giving yourself an appraisal and also having a review meeting with yourself. Having someone to bounce ideas off is crucial. Remember the section under Meetings about Business Review Meetings? Let it be said that having a meeting with yourself does feel like heading towards madness. I have never felt more of a prat than doing my annual review. And I have a quarterly review coming up. No doubt the cat will have to stand in as trusted advisor.

Local business hubs

It is well worth checking out any local enterprise schemes where you live. This may not be as easy as it sounds as local government and local council websites seem to be built to create confusion but persevere. Bumping into them well after I needed them, I blew that option, but they can offer some great stuff. If you can track them down (and there may be several varieties where you live), there is usually something in each area that is set up specifically to help newly created small businesses. That can be anything from drop in sessions for free with an accountant or mentoring or free networking. The main benefit of this is that it is either free or very cheap and it is a good way of making local connections. Near me, you join and you can rent meetings rooms for free in the local hub and work in the drop-in centre (ace for when the broadband packs up, saves a fortune in Chai Lattes in Costa).

Money, money, money

Disclaimer

I quite freely admit that I am numerically terrified. If there is one area to take advice on in business it's money, especially tax. If you cock up, HMRC are not known for their forgiving natures. So, if you are unsure, for the love of all that is Holy, check with someone. Someone that isn't me. Ta.

Invoicing

It is quite exciting when you send out your first invoice as a proper self-employed person. It's even better when it gets paid! The novelty of this does wear off eventually (it only took a few months). Basically, as soon as I compared my little invoices to my ex-salary I became miserable and jaded and decided that one invoice a month better be put aside for a gin fund. In actual fact, I really don't like sending invoices. Which is stupid. Because everyone knows they are coming and fully expects them. I do have a tendency to agonise over sending them at different times. On a Monday morning (because Monday mornings are shit enough without a bill arriving). Or Friday afternoon (because people are all about the pub). I had one client tell me off for apologising for sending an invoice at all! A few years on and I'm over it. Once I move to my online accounting system it will do it for me (and send reminders, and thank people as they pay) and that will make me happy. One step removed. One great little tip on the mindset of rates is to describe them as "the rates" rather than "my rates". It makes it less personal. It's the same thing as getting a system to send invoices – it makes it feel more businessy and less like you asking for money!

The million-dollar question

Hilariously, when I set up I thought I could work out my rates by doing annual salary divided by fifty-two weeks divided by forty hours. Or some such lunacy (I was in the pub at the time on a Friday night, that's my only excuse). Happily, a friend VA gently explained to me that if I did that I would likely be in the workhouse in about a month. Freelance rates are not the same as employee rates. They are not! If you want to earn what you did before (and still sleep) then you will need to charge appropriately. There are lots of ways of working this out just don't try it my way! Yes, it sounds like a lot when you first hear it. Sense check it with a trusted UK VA trainer if you are aren't sure or send me a message and I'll suggest some people to talk to. Remember this has to cover your work time AND your sales time, admin time, holidays, sickness, equipment, repairs, insurance and other bloody things HRMC and Data Protection expect you to fork out for as well as the light, heat and teabags for your office. Oh, and pens. Every VA needs nice pens and a notebook – stationery is now a business expense so fill your boots!

Spending it to make it

It's an interesting shift in mindset once you run a business. There are expenses. Depending on how and why you set up, you may have more spare cash or less spare cash. Be aware, you will need to spend money! Not necessarily on everything but there are expenses when you run a business.

You will be forking out for networking events, software, IT, training. You have to factor this into your rates and your cashflow.

You will be making decisions about budgets and how to spend them. If you really want your business to succeed then you are most likely going to have to invest some money by spending it on the business – whether that is training for you or a new PC.

Keeping books

There are lots of very whizzy systems to manage your accounts if you want to use them. I love Xero and Free Agent. Zoho is another popular one. But, in the early days you can save your pennies and use a good old fashioned spreadsheet if you so choose.

The main things you need to record are your invoices to clients, when they are paid(!), your expenditure and also mileage for work if you go out and about. The self-assessment doesn't break down expenses into particular categories but you can if helps you.

You'll need to keep copies of all receipts and a log of any mileage you are claiming as a business expense.

I know it sounds like the worst way to spend forty-five minutes ever and you'd rather staple your nipples to the nearest desk, but it is worth checking out the HMRC resources online. I attended a great webinar about what expenses are billable and how to work out your working at home cost (you can charge for that!) and they also have webinars on how to do self-assessments. It's a free resource and definitely worth a look.

Keep calm and do a self-assessment

This was one area of freelance life I was totally dreading. Scary tax shit is high up on my fear list. And do you know what? It was fine. Totally fine.

I am registered as self-employed and as my business is just me – I am a sole trader. Some VAs do set up limited companies. Not being an accountant I can give no advice on what's best, but so far, sole trader is working ok for me.

As far as I can see, the biggest mistake people make with a self-assessment, is leaving it to the last minute. The tax year ends March (ish, April the whatever) and you don't have to submit the self-assessment until around Christmas. Insane. How the hell can you remember that far back if you have a problem? Also, to my mind, the sooner you know how much tax you have to pay, gulp, the sooner you can make sure you have it! So, I do my self-assessment in the summer when it's quiet. I book a day and just do it. Last year I booked lunch and self-assessment with my dad at my place – that way there was no escape. We both got our self-assessments done and had a nice lunch at mine. You don't even need to submit it in one go, you can sit and look at it for a few months before pressing the button if that appeals but at least you know. Right?

As long as you have accurate records, the actual online bit is a piece of piss. The most traumatic bit of my most recent experience was trying to track down my Government Gateway reference number which I had put in such a safe place I couldn't find the bastard thing at all. In the time it took me to ransack my office for this bit of paper, my dad had finished his entire self-assessment and made a coffee. That will teach me not to be smug and naggy after I reminded my poor father, rather patronisingly, seventeen times "don't forget that special Gateway thing". And after all that, the number was exactly where it should have been in my password protected, password document!

All you really need is records of your income. All varieties thereof, so employment, unemployment, self-employment. As long as you keep your P60s you're grand and then you'll tot up your invoices. Any bank interest (ha!), stocks and shares and so on. It's pretty simply laid out.

Then you do the same with your outgoings. The only thing I was asked and had no record of was charitable donations. I now make a note of these. I don't think they're deductible but maybe it's a gift aid thing.

You don't pay tax on things you have to buy, your expenditure comes off your turnover to give you profit you only pay tax on profit.

But, you will have to pay tax! This should be obvious but somehow it can still come as a surprise. One of the most useful bits of business advice I got when setting up was to automatically put 40% of my income into an account ready for the tax bill. HMRC will get you to pay some in advance once you are into your second year so you really do need to have some money put by in readiness.

If you are truly terrified, you can have a book-keeper or accountant to either do this for you or check it once you've done it before you submit it. But, take it from a numerical numpty, give it a try first in plenty of time and see how you get on before paying someone to do it for you.

Working at home

One of the things that people really want from being a VA is to work at home. The sheer luxury of not having to commute somewhere, battling trains, traffic jams and sweaty armpits on the tube is enough to make people think that working from home, doing more or less anything at all, is a good call. And it is! I used to commute into London every day and now I move about ten foot to my study and I can more or less skip the makeup. It is a far cry from the corporate world and whilst that has many many advantages, it also does have its challenges. But let's ignore those for now and luxuriate in all that is brilliant about being a homeworker...

You can wear your pyjamas to the office. By and large. The popularity of video calls, Google Hangouts, Zoom, Skype etc is on the rise and I have one client who always does a video call. I don't think of myself as being particularly dim but I have struggled to remember this so much that I have now scheduled his calls after a networking meeting so that I am a) dressed and b) wearing a bit of makeup. I also need to be at home ideally so I can control the environment to a degree. And I need to look behind me to check the state of the office. I have collie with a bin fetish so often end up with the bin on top of the printer, it doesn't look great! Also, closing the door to hide my knickers drying on the suspended washing line is a good move. See, you don't have to fret about this kind of thing when you just rock up to an office do you? I also have to remind myself when on a video call that gestures can be seen! On audio meetings you can get away with a lot. I mean a lot. Painting your nails, knocking up a bit of soup – assuming you are only a partial attendee of course. I wouldn't recommend either of those with clients, paying attention is quite key. But my point is, that on an audio you can, if needed, communicate with those around you. This might be a simple finger over the lips, shhh, or a quick hit of the mute button and a loud "Shuuuut up! I'm on a call". Or, as one VA friend regaled, the old finger across the throat, glower and snarl technique at her kids who were playing up. And this is where it all falls down – she had the video on. So her client saw her facial expressions and the gesture and burst out laughing. I am no better. Whilst on video (with brain in audio mode) I have had the dog climb on my lap, left the room(!) and turned the sound off and waved frantically at my mum whilst shouting "mum, shhh, I'm on a call with a client". Said client did his best not to laugh and then confessed he could read my lips. I don't work from my parents' house any more after that incident. Or if I did, I'd probably lock myself in the loo to do a Skype!

So yes, working from home is great. You can put on a load of laundry, be in for the gas man and look like a homeless person without anyone realising. Knickers are optional and if you have a stinking cold you can work from under the covers.

Discipline

I know, I know. The minute you start working for yourself from home you want to get up about 10.00am, rock up to your desk about 11.00am and finish by 2.00pm. Oh, me too. So much. But in reality, if I want to earn enough money I have to be a bit more energetic than that! Which is a pity. My dream working hours are Monday and Wednesday 10.00am until about 11.00am. I'll be sure to write another book and tell you how I manage to pull that off. I will have plenty of time as by then I will be mostly living in Rio, drinking cocktails by the pool. Hmmm.

And the opposite can happen too. You find yourself basically working whenever you aren't asleep. This is a real danger especially if you live on your own. And it is just as bad for your health (and then, inevitably your finances). If you never take a break you will eventually burn out and end up a sobbing little mess in the corner. You can suddenly realise that you haven't actually left your desk since 6am except to pee and make coffee and you have yet to clean your teeth. I know of one VA who realised that she didn't leave her house for five days at a stretch! This is not healthy! She went and got a dog, now she has to leave the house. I highly recommend dogs as a means to getting out of the building and also talking to actual real people – something you miss in the virtual world. There is a real need when you work at home to set boundaries otherwise work and life melds in together and you are neither off nor on at any point. So I get round that by mostly doing a 9am -5pm (8am – 6pm), something that resembles a normal working day and then walking away from the PC. I might come back to it later. When stuff just needs doing I do have late nights sometimes, as you do in any job. But it is the exception and not the rule. The same for "faffing in front of the TV".

Faffing in front of the TV is one of my worst habits. It means that either I am not fully paying attention to what I am doing or, more likely, have no clue what is happening on screen. So what is the point? I don't know. Sometimes it is nice not to be at my desk! When I am doing my own stuff, writing blogs, updating my CRM and so on, it seems silly to be in my office. And I do like a change of scene. But basically it means I can't watch anything with subtitles ever. Or in fact anything with a plot I have to follow. Which limits me to light comedy or dross I don't care about which basically makes me think, what's the point? I'd be better off at my desk as I am not actually watching this.

I have a friend who has Netflix on the go while she works and has done three series of Game of Thrones! How? It's one of the few things I actually pay attention to and at times I still haven't the foggiest idea who's fighting who. And she has a very important job which she is very good at. I must go and learn how to pull this off. For me, I have to either work with music or the radio on fairly quietly, or TV that I have seen before or I don't care about. Because I know I'm not paying attention properly, I'm just not.

So basically, I work what most people would call a normal work day. And I take a lunch hour. If I can occasionally get to my desk at 7am and get a couple of hours under my belt then I am very happy. Some nights I end up at the desk later than I'd like, that's life. But I don't (anymore!) get up, stagger to the laptop in my PJs and start work.

I do the odd bit at a weekend, at the very least I do my planning for the following week so I know what is going on when. My present version of this involves a monthly bit of paper with my client hours on so I know how many I need to book and for whom, my Todoist task app, a printed off schedule for the whole week in half hour slots and a large set of colourful pencils. Sunday night sees me doing my colouring. I may not always stick rigidly to the plan but I know once it is done where I have wriggle room and where I don't. I try not to do client work at the weekend but if I have my own bits to do – writing, planning, a particular campaign I am working on for my business, then I'll do that.

Lunch hours I love

It is SO important for me to take a proper break in the middle of the day. It doesn't need to be lunch either, that's the joy of self-employment, I could take my "lunch" break at 11am or 3pm if I wanted. And sometimes I do. And it doesn't have to be an hour. I try never to make it less than half an hour but it is sometimes more. Again, feel the flexibility!

Normally, lunch consists of getting out with the dogs for an hour. But if I don't do that then there are many many other things that I can and have used my lunch hour for:

- Cleaning the house
- Doing some ironing (seriously rare, I'd have to be avoiding something pretty horrific to stoop to this level)
- Collecting stuff from somewhere, shopping
- Bit of crochet
- Reading a book
- Dog walk or lunch with friends
- Unbunging the washing machine filter
- Building a flat pack bed
- Mowing the lawn
- Personal training session at the gym or home
- Napping

Anyway, you get the point. Whilst some of these are not in the least fun, they are at least different to sitting staring at a screen and involve a change of scenery. That's the key for me.

Other people (are very annoying)

Left to my own devices, I am very good at being organised, hitting my billable hours target and generally being an efficient and calm human. But what can throw a spanner in these works is other people. And more specifically, what other people think working at home means.

People think that because you are at home you are available. I'm not talking about clients although goodness knows some of them do seem to think I sit by the phone twiddling my thumbs waiting for the phone to ring so I can work on their stuff. I'm talking friends, family and others. As the only homeworker in your circle you pretty soon become the one who "does stuff". I know that when you are in an office it can be difficult to be the one who gets on the concert ticket website when it opens and constantly refreshes until getting through, so it seems like sense to delegate to the person sitting at home in private. Ditto booking restaurants, events and so on by phone. But we have to work! If you are an office worker and you pop to Costa to pick up a latte you are still paid for that. Me, not so much. You still get paid for your twelve minutes to nip out, I don't.

The best one I get is "can you pick us up from the airport?" Now, of an evening, a weekend, even at shit o'clock in the morning that is OK. I am a noble soul. 2pm on a weekday? That's my afternoon gone people. But I am not yet brave enough to have the conversation that says "It would cost you £30 to get a cab, for me to come and get you has likely cost me £100 or so of earnings". This does not factor into people's minds. They just kind of think we can do the work later. Well maybe we can. Maybe we can't. Would you ask someone working in an office in a "normal job" to pick you up and then go back to work until 8pm? No, you wouldn't. If you are thinking of becoming a VA I suggest you go to the Billable Hours section and copy it for your loved ones. Print it out and stick chunks on the fridge. Because every time they say "can you just..." precious minutes leach out of your working life.

Can you just get my dry cleaning? Can you just pop to the post office for that special delivery letter? Can you just, can you just? No I bloody can't, I am trying to earn a living here!

And in the same way, the house doesn't miraculously get itself clean now that you are at home. I know you thought it would. But it just doesn't happen like that.

Washing has seen an improvement since I worked at home. I can fit in loads in and out at the same time as a wee and cup of tea and that works for me. Although, on at least three occasions I have put a load of washing in at 7am and completely forgotten about it until I knock off at 5.30pm.

Nothing throws a spanner in a perfectly planned day like another person. And BT. BT can put a spanner in any day. Even a person being nice. The old, "oh, are you in, I'll pop round with that article, Tupperware dish, random shit". Because at the least you have to answer the door and if they look set to stay, you have to make them a coffee and talk to them. Again, would you pop into your mate's place of work if you happen to drive past the industrial estate? No, probably not. Maybe if they owned the company and had a really good coffee machine, but you wouldn't know if they had meetings or a deadline or whatever. When you work at home people don't think these things are as important. You are at home and therefore you are available for doing stuff. Even if you actually aren't.

So how do you manage this? Well, it depends on who you are dealing with really. I discourage people from coming to the house. If I want a social, I'll meet them elsewhere and give a time when I need to be back for a call. If people tell me they are going to drop off something then I will either tell them I can't stop work, have a Skype call booked (conveniently five minutes after their ETA) or that if they could make it at X time I could stop for a coffee. In a dire emergency I might tell them to leave the something outside. Because I have dogs who do a superb job of protecting me from well-meaning folk delivering things, anyone coming to the door for any reason is a nightmare if I am on the phone or whatever. I can get properly irate at these people who are usually only being nice but who don't realise I am actually on page fifty six of a sixty-page webinar recording which I will now have to start again because they have interrupted me. Interrupted me and started the domestic dog equivalent of a call to arms. Just to ask if they can have their Betterware catalogue back. Yes, fucking take it. It's three inches to your left on top of the recycle bin, SO YOU COULD TAKE IT WITHOUT RINGING THE DAMN BELL. Thank you for utterly fucking up my morning you dickwad. I know, it is unreasonable to expect people to know that I am doing these things and would be much better if I could train the damn dogs not to howl the place down when the chance of a microwave egg poacher is imminent, but I can't. I could drug them I guess. If I have an absolutely crucial call at what is normal Gordon the postman time I have been known to lock myself in the car or them in the garden (but then you just get them yipping to come in and I have yet to work out which is the most offensive noise. Perhaps a Google form client questionnaire in due course? "Which would you say is most annoying a) barking b) howling c) yipping or d) scratching noises that sound like a zombie trying to dig itself out of a grave.") Or I could build myself a log cabin at the end of the garden and hide in there. That way I would really never remember to put the washing out and I wouldn't see the mess in the rest of the house. It's a plan!

But really, it is difficult when people have no idea that you are trying to work and run a business from home. I'd love to be more flexible and just drop everything and go to the coffee shop. I pretty much thought that's what I was buying into. But I just don't seem to be able to fit that in somehow! Which leads nicely on to the next section.

How not to be a hermit (bra wearing and other non-negotiables)

A woman on an online discussion board once said "well, it's 3pm now and I haven't put a bra on yet so there's really no point".

Now I am all for the non-wearing of bras and if I am going nowhere (and have no video calls!) might opt for the bra-free look. But, it is a slippery slope from not bothering with underwear, to wearing "lounge wear" (God help us) to skipping showers for a few days, not getting dressed at all and then a slow descent into something really quite minging and not very nice at all. Think geeky gamer who has done a few all-nighters at the screen. That is what the end game is. It's not pretty is it?

I get around this potential slippage by having dogs. They have to go out twice a day or they systematically destroy the house around me which makes noise, which stops me working. They also usually start with pens and I am very fond of pens and stationery in general so keeping them at a level of tiredness is good for them, good for me and good for my pen stash. It is a good discipline. It is great for me because I get exercise, fresh air and usually meet actual other humans in person. This is important. I know homeworkers who traumatise their local shopkeepers by talking to them at top speed for twenty-five minutes as they realise it is the only face to face human contact they have had in seventy-two hours. This isn't healthy! Plus, your local shopkeeper is also trying to run a business and, like us, doesn't need some nutter wasting their time. I know video chats, Skypes, blah. Face to face human stuff is important. If you don't have a dog but quite like them you can borrow someone else's. I loan mine out on a site called Borrow my Doggy and they have a wonderful time (and I can fit in more billable hours!). Or at the least make sure you do a proper lunch hour out of the building every day which means you will need to be wearing actual clothing.

I have one friend who sometimes comes and works at my house. We each do our own thing, head down and then go for a walk and a natter at lunchtime. I also do working sessions with a client in a local coffee shop – we both enjoy the company even though there is no real need for us to be in the same room to do the work. On occasion, we even do a virtual working session, just doing our own work with but with Skype on. She finds it keeps her from getting distracted and I'm doing the work either way so I don't much care. But it's kind of sociable. I know another VA who goes and hot desks in someone else's office a couple of days a week. Largely, I think that is escaping from her children, but it is still company as you would get in a regular job. And you have to have a shower and put on proper clothes.

It does depend on your living situation. If you live with five other people then eight hours of solid aloneness might be your idea of heaven. But for some people, working alone isn't fun and they find it hard. It's rare that I am not motivated to get on with things (a dull level of panic will do that to you!) but some people really find it miserable. I can struggle to do my own work. Client work takes priority and then by the time I get to my own I can't really be arsed and because it's mine it doesn't feel that urgent. After all, the boss sets deadlines, I am the boss and what I say goes! Even if that is "ah, fuck it, tomorrow's fine".

So, I plan to see people, I arrive at my desk mostly showered and wearing underwear and clothes I could be seen in public in and I always leave the house at least once a day. Those are my non-negotiables.

Dog heaven and dog hell

More or less the first thing I did when I started working at home was get a puppy. I've always wanted a dog but the hours I worked out of the house had meant that wasn't possible. So, once I had my working from home job (this was before I became self-employed) and it looked set to continue, puppy number one arrived.

The best thing about having dogs is that they do not tolerate lack of exercise. For my sanity, they are the best thing ever because even in the filthiest of weathers they have to go out. They are also lovely company, I do my afternoon work with one curled up on my feet and the other one behind me. I can talk to them and they don't answer back. What's not to like?

Well. It has its moments! My dogs (puppy #2 arrived a few years after puppy #1) are both capable of embarrassing me both inside and outside of the house. There is the daily insane barking when Gordon the postman delivers. If anyone walks past the house (I happily live in a fairly remote place but it does happen) they will protect it to the death. God forbid a plumber is allowed next door, the cheek! All of which is fine until you are on a call or a Skype with someone important and it sounds like you are living in a kennels. Most people are sympathetic but it isn't ideal. I spend quite a bit of time on mute.

Mabel (puppy #2) has also been known to leap up onto my desk. One time she also knocked my laptop to the floor – killing it. Dead. The utter horror of being without any form of laptop is indescribable. My laptop was fixable it turned out. New hard drive. I tried and failed to pay the nice IT man with a cute but ludicrously naughty Border Collie....

Then there is the joy of being on a call and knowing, just knowing, that the dog is up to something but you can't make a gracious escape to go and sort it out. Once on a call I could hear peculiar noises from the kitchen. Engrossed as I was with my call, I couldn't help but wonder what on earth was going on. So, I took my mobile off speaker, picked it up and went downstairs with it…. Damn dog had leapt onto the work surface to steal something out of the food waste bin. In the process, she'd managed to knock a few things on the floor and turn the kitchen tap on full blast which was hammering loudly against a baking tray in the sink and spraying water up the walls and down onto the floor. I think it is a credit to my cool, calm exterior that my colleague knew nothing about any of this as I carried on our conversation whilst mopping the floor and picking up strawberry tops.

And having dogs in a way is a bit like having kids. I had to tell my old boss I couldn't do a client meeting once because of the dog (Puppy #1 that time). She had eaten a lightbulb and I had to watch her for 24 hours in case anything ruptured. No way was I leaving that dog! And if I go and work onsite with clients, which I do quite often as I enjoy a change in scenery, I have to find a dog sitter or a dog walker depending on how long I'm out. And those flaky clients that change their minds at the 11th hour don't realise that much like child care, these things have to be organised ahead of time and can't always be moved at the drop of a hat. And they cost money. Sometimes I do a day with a client who isn't on the best rate and I have to work for an hour before I've covered the dog walker.

But, laptop deaths, tap explosions and barking aside, having dogs is the best thing for me about working at home. And I wouldn't change it for the world.

I'll just perch here – workspaces to make or break you

I made a few mistakes when I started working at home. Not least of which was my equipment and set up. I've been lucky enough to always have a spare room to work in, but if I tell you that I used to work eight hours a day on a £6.00 canvas wheelie chair from Argos… My goodness. I don't know how I functioned. Eventually the pain in my arse (actual arse ache!) made me change to a proper office chair and proper desk but I did ten months on a set that is designed for a small child to do finger painting on.

I know people that work all day every day on the sofa, or a dining room table. How?! Firstly, think of your posture! Sitting for lengthy periods is bad enough anyway but sitting on something that isn't designed for long term use is a fast track to breaking yourself. I know it's a right pain to be forking out money for kit in the initial stages but it does have to be done.

Ideally, life is better if you can have a dedicated space with a desk, a few shelves, a pot plant if you want to call your office. Psychologically, it is good to walk in and think "I am now at work" and to run out at the end of the day "I'm outta here". It keeps some nice boundaries time wise and also space wise. I keep a pretty clear desk but I have one client who, having filled his work office with paper has now filled not one, but TWO living rooms at home with work stuff. He just doesn't do throwing things away so he'll just keep expanding until the whole house is full. He'll probably have piles of paper stashed under the kids' beds in a few years and his wife will find him one day behind a stack of lever arch files unable to escape. (I should point out here that it is not for lack of trying on my part that he has all this paper. I do rather feel I have failed as a VA on this! I spent days, and I mean, DAYS scanning documents, so he could throw things away. He didn't. In my latest attempt to manage the paper mountain I sorted piles of stuff and had a "To Shred" bag. Which, after I left, he went through and decided he needed all of, even though 80% of it was scribbled notes and duplicate copies of meeting agendas from 2014. At this point I feel a VA isn't needed so much as a therapist. Short of sneaking it out of his house (tempting) and binning it, there is no way to remove any paper, no matter how trivial from this bloke's life).

Anyway, assuming you do not have paper hoarding tendencies and you can keep a space tidy, then a corner of a room is OK. But you don't want your work there in your face at all times. If you can't keep it tidy or hidden and it bugs you (or your nearest and dearest) then you may need to come up with a plan to create some designated space. A garden room, loft conversation or even a shed!

And in this space, you really should have a proper office chair. And a proper keyboard and mouse if you use a laptop. Even better, a big screen or (and there is research on the improvements in productivity of doing this) two screens, even three screens. Yes, pretend like you're bank trader. Once you have had two screens going back to one will be like going back to a dial up modem. If you are a full-time home worker, you need professional kit.

And on that subject. Broadband. There's that old rhyme – when it's good it's really good but when it's bad it's awful. That is homeworking with broadband. Bar the collie / laptop incident, broadband traumas are the one thing that have nearly brought me to my knees as a VA. Because we're all the in the cloud and that's brilliant for when your laptop hits the floor at 50mph so you don't lose your life's work, but totally frigging useless if your Wi-Fi runs like an asthmatic dog. As are Skype calls and Google Hangouts. Then you realise that your printer is also on the Wi-Fi network so that's out of action as well! What works really well for faffing on Facebook of an evening plus a bit of Netflix, might not be up to scratch to work fulltime with, so it's really important to get a decent service. I have a VA friend who is moving house to a new area and will not move to any location without fibre optic broadband or Virgin Media. It's that vital. And I know we can up sticks and go work anywhere… but you still have to get it fixed if it breaks, which takes time (and depending on your provider: much wine and Valium and not a few expletives) and usually has to be done in the house (where you now can't actually work).

AND FINALLY

So, if you aren't already a VA I do hope this book hasn't entirely put you off the idea!

It is a brilliant way to earn a living. Now that you know some of the things that might throw a spanner in the works you can at least decide if it sounds like the right path for you.

If you do decide to go ahead, get some support. Come and find me, www.facebook.com/VirtuallyPainlessVA or @virtuallypainls on Twitter and say "hi".

And a HUGE favour. If you've enjoyed this book, or even bits of this book, **please, please, please** write a review on Amazon. Go and do it right now before you forget. Everyone buys these days based on reviews, they are so important. You will have my endless gratitude!

ABOUT THE AUTHOR

Prior to becoming a VA, Kathy Soulsby worked for over fifteen years as a PA, EA and Office Manager for various firms in London and the South East. She set up her VA business in October 2014 and by July 2015 was working in the business fulltime.

The dream was that free from the corporate machine, her freelance days would be spent sitting in fabulous coffee shops with a sleek laptop, the house would be clean, she'd be far less stressed with no boss and she could now pop to the gym any time she fancied. The reality turned out to be more, well, real.

Kathy has had to learn how to find clients, how to negotiate, how to take on associates, how to do her own books and how to position a laptop for a Skype call so clients can't see her washing drying over the stairs. Mainly, she has learnt that there was a great deal she didn't have a clue about before embarking on this way of life which it might have been good to know beforehand. That was inspiration for this book – filling in the blanks. There was plenty of information on how to set up and what to do, but the reality of the experience and how it feels came as rather a surprise.

Professionally, Kathy is a founding member of VIP VA, a group started to stringently vet and champion excellent Virtual Assistants and their huge contribution to business and the UK economy. She is a mentor to a fledgling VA and regularly offers advice to new VAs setting up. When not sweating over an electronic timesheet, she can be found running around local fields doing flyball, agility and many many walks with her two collies so they don't eat her favourite pens.

ACKNOWLEDGEMENTS

This book is dedicated to all the PAs, EAs and VAs out there doing an amazing job.

A huge thank you to everyone who has inspired and encouraged me to write this book and to all those who have supported my VA journey so far. I am very lucky to be surrounded by amazing people both in business and in my personal life. I am more grateful than I can ever say to each and every one of you; for the kind words, the kicks up the arse, the looking after of dogs (so I can work) and, of course, the supply of gin!

Printed in Great Britain
by Amazon